Beyond Blend Phonics

A Natural and Easy Method
for Teaching Advanced English Morphology
Through the Languages of Origin

By Donald L. Potter

DEDICATION

To all my tutoring students over the last twenty years
who motivated me to do my best
so they could be a success

CONTENTS

Acknowledgments

Beyond Blend Phonics

ACKNOWLEDGMENTS

Dr. Earl Eugene Roth, Jr.

For encouraging me to teach English morphemes
in order to increase students' reading skills.

Dr. Marcia K. Henry

Past President of the International Dyslexia Society

For helping me understand how to improve student reading, spelling and
composition by organizing decoding instruction
according to the language of origin.

Dr. George González

Professor of ESL and Bilingual Education at the
University of Texas, Pan American, Edinburg, TX.,

For teaching me how to teach vocabulary through parallel sentences:
We teach **vocabulary**. We help students learn the *meanings of words*.

Chapter 1

Anglo-Saxon **Prefixes**

Anglo-Saxon English
From the Days of King Arthur
and the Knights of the Round Table

for-

1-1. for·get´: I will never **forget** you. I will remember you forever.

1-2. for·bid´: I **forbid** you to eat chocolate in class. I will *not let* you eat chocolate in class.

1-3. for·give´: I **forgive** you for eating my chocolate. I will *not be upset* with you for eating my chocolate since you said you were sorry and promised never to do it again.

1-4. fore·close´: They will **foreclose** on Marina's house today. They will *take away* the house because she could not make the monthly payments.

1-5. for·sake´: Do not **forsake** your best friends. Do not *leave* your best friends but always be faithful and true to them.

be-

1-6. be·cause´: You cannot go outside **because** it is raining. The *reason* you cannot go outside is that you will get wet in the rain.

1-7. be·came´: John studied a lot and **became** a good student. He *got to be* real smart.

1-8. be·friend´: You should **befriend** new students at your school. You should *become their friend*.

1-9. be·hold´: **Behold** the good work Sarah did for her teacher. *Look carefully at* the good work Sarah did for her teacher.

1-10. **be·siege′:** The army **besieged** the enemy's city. They *surrounded it and wouldn't let anyone in or out* until the city surrendered.

1-11. **be·hind′:** My black dog is **behind** the couch. He is *in back of* the couch and doesn't want to come out.

in-

1-12. **in′to:** I don't want to go **into** the dark house. I don't know what might be in there. **Into** is a preposition.

1-13. **in·side′:** You have to read the book to know what is **inside.** You have to open it and take a look.

over-

1-14. **o·ver·look′:** The house **overlooked** the river. The house was built high up on the hill so people could *have a view from above* and see the river below. It can also mean to *fail to notice.* Don't *over look* the important fact. Don't *miss* it.

1-15. **o·ver·come′:** By hard work, you can **overcome** great problems. You can *solve problems* so they don't get you down.

1-16. **o·ver·bear′ing:** The shop foreman was **overbearing.** He bossed everyone around and never listened to what they had to say.

1-17. **o·ver·worked′:** The farmer was **overworked.** He was tired because he worked all the time and never took any time off to rest. He *worked too much.*

with-

1-18. with·out´: You cannot get into the movie theater **without** a ticket. You cannot get into the movie theater if you *do not have* a ticket *with you.*

1-19. with·stand´: The house was designed to **withstand** a strong earthquake. It will *not fall down* no matter how much the earth moves. It *offers strong resistance* to the storm.

1-20. with·hold´: Jerry's parents decided to **withhold** their son's allowance until he did his homework. They *held it back* until he did his work.

by-

1-21. by´stan·der: The **bystander** was not allowed on the baseball diamond. He could only *stand by* and watch.

1-22. by´line: I saw Jim's name in the newspaper **byline**. That is how I knew he wrote the article. A **byline** is *a line in a newspaper naming the writer of the article.*

un-
(not)

1-23. un·hap´py: Sally was very **unhappy** because she lost her purple purse with the diamond on the side. She was *not happy.*

1-24. un·like´: The car was **unlike** any I had ever seen before. It was *not like* any I had seen before because it was a metallic purple.

1-25. **un·like′ly:** It was **unlikely** that we would ever see a real lion in our house. It is *not likely* that a lion would get along with my dad's elephant.

1-26. **un·hap′pi·ly: Unhappily** my dad's elephant stepped on my baby lion. I was *not happy* when Dad's elephant stepped on my baby lion.

1-27. **un·will′ing:** My brother was **unwilling** to mow the lawn. He *did not want to* mow it, but Dad made him mow it anyway.

1-28. **un·kind′ly:** Jack spoke **unkindly** to my little brother because he spilled his milk. Jack yelled and was *not kind* to my little brother when he spilled his milk.

1-29. **un·nerv′ing:** John said his fall on his bike was **unnerving**. He was so scared that he didn't want to ride again for a long time. He *lost his nerve*.

1-30. **un·re·served′:** We sat in the **unreserved** section at the football game. The seats were *not reserved* because no one had saved them.

1-31. **un·de·ser′ving:** Henry was **undeserving** of the grade he got on his essay about Russia. He did *not deserve* it because he just copied an article from an encyclopedia.

under-

1-32. **un·der·stand′:** I did not **understand** a word Henry said about his new dog. I did not *comprehend* what he was talking about.

1-33. un·der·go´: I had to **undergo** surgery on my jaw years ago to remove an infected tooth. I had to suffer through uncomfortable surgery.

1-34. un·der·went´: Jerry **underwent** surgery for a shoulder he hurt in a football game. He was *subject to* the procedure.

1-35. un·der·age´: My little sister Mary is **underage**. She is *under the age* that they allow on the big rides at the fair.

1-36. un·der·stu´dy: Jaxon Santos is Mr. Potter's **understudy**. He is *studying under* Mr. Potter's direction at OCS to teach his friends in first grade to read better.

a-

1-37. a·like´: Walter and Mable Potter's twin boys look **alike**. They *look exactly the same*. One was Mr. Potter's dad!

1-38. a·mount´: He gave me the exact **amount**. He gave me the correct change. Amount means "how much."

1-39. a·ground´: After the terrible storm, the ship found itself **aground** on the beach. It was *stuck* on the beach and couldn't be moved.

1-40. a·round´: Is there any money **around** here? Do we have any money *near by*.

1-41. a·bout´: There are **about** thirty people in the room. There are *more or less* thirty people in the room. I am not exactly sure because I haven't counted them.

Chapter 2

Anglo-Saxon **Suffixes**

Anglo-Saxon English
From the days of King Arthur
and the Knights of the Round Table

-ed
(past tense)

2-1. **walked:** My Dad **walked** to school every day. That was in the past, a long time ago.

2-2. **hoped:** I **hoped** that Dad would buy me a bicycle for my birthday. I *wanted* him to buy me a bicycle.

2-3. **hopped:** A grey rabbit **hopped** merrily down the path. He *jumped up and down* happily.

2-4. **skipped:** The little boy **skipped** down the rocky path. He was *jumping with little steps* from rock to rock.

2-5. **bat·ted:** Jimmy **batted** one-hundred at the ball game yesterday. He *hit the ball* every time and never missed.

2-6. **pat·ted:** Lucy lovingly **patted** her little yellow cat. She would pat him gently on the head.

-er -ar -or
(agent: someone doing something)

2-7. **pain´ter:** The **painter** painted a beautiful painting of a beautiful waterfall. A **painter** is *someone who paints.*

2-8. **wri´ter:** The **writer** wrote a fantastic novel about two brave policemen helping people. A writer is *one who writes.*

2-9. **far´mer:** The hardworking **farmer** planted one-hundred acres of popcorn. A farmer is *one who farms* the land.

2-10. **work′er:** My Dad was a **worker** on a dairy farm. He milked Guernsey cows. A worker is *one who works*.

2-11. **schol′ar:** Jim is a really smart **scholar**. He studies hard and makes good grades a school. A scholar is *one who studies*.

2-12. **auth′or:** Jane is an **author** of a good book on manners for children. She *wrote a book* to teach children how to be nice to others. Authors *write stories and books*.

-hood
(condition, state, quality)

2-13. **state′hood:** Indiana was a territory before it obtained **statehood.** It was just a territory before Congress decided to let it become *recognized as a state*.

2-14. **bro′ther·hood:** We believe in the **brotherhood** of all humankind. We are all brothers and sisters of one another in this world.

2-15. **sis′ter·hood:** My sisters believe in **sisterhood**. They do everything together as sisters.

2-16. **knight′hood: Knighthood** was the code of honor for the knights during the Middle Ages. The brave knights worked together to protect the beautiful princesses

-ing
Present Participle

2-17. **walk′ing: Walking** is good for your health. When you keep your feet moving, you are exercising your heart, lungs, and body.

2-18. **fly´ing: Flying** an airplane is a good way to get somewhere fast. Jets fly really fast.

2-19. **talk´ing: Talking** is very important. Learning to talk clearly and accurately will help you make better grades at school and get a better job when you graduate.

-ful
(full)

2-20. **aw´ful:** I had an **awful** headache yesterday. My head hurt a lot. It was a *terrible* headache.

2-21. **care´ful:** You need to be **careful** when you cross a street. Be sure and look both ways and make sure no cars are coming. You should be *full of care* when crossing a busy street.

2-22. **fear´ful:** We were **fearful** of the strange dog running down the street. We stayed in the house because we were *full of fear.*

2-23. **tear´ful:** We were **tearful** because our best friend moved away. Our eyes were *full of tears* when their car pulled off. We will miss them a lot.

2-24. **use´ful:** A pencil is very **useful.** You can use a pencil to write all kinds of things like poems, stories, novels, biographies, and friendly letters. It is *full of uses.*

2-25. **help´ful:** An dictionary is very **helpful** if you need to know how to spell a word or find out what it means. A dictionary is *full of help.*

2-26. **hope´ful:** I am very **hopeful** that I will get a Red Racer bicycle for my birthday. I *am full of hope* that I will get one.

-less
(without, lacking)

2-27. **help´less:** Maria was **helpless** when it came to baking a cake. She needed lots of help from her mother.

2-28. **sense´less:** Jim fell off his horse and was knocked **senseless** when his head hit the ground. He woke up later and was fine when his senses came back.

2-29. **use´less:** Harry was **useless** at football. He could not run, throw, tackle, or catch. It was *no use* to even try. He played basketball instead.

2-30. **hope´less:** It is **hopeless** to try to get a 100% at spelling without studying. There is *no hope* at all if you don't study.

-s, -es
(plural, more than one)

2-31. **dogs:** Jim has one boy dog and two girl **dogs**. I put the letter *s* at the end of *dog* to show that there is more than one girl dog. The *s* makes a singular word plural.

2-32. **cars:** I have had a lot of **cars** in my life. I once owned a 1960 Thunderbird. It was a pretty blue car. It was too fast so I sold it.

2-33. **rooms:** There are many **rooms** in the White House. The President and his wife live there.

2-34. **fox´es:** Red **foxes** live in the forest. Add the letters *es* instead of just the letter *s* at the end of words ending in *x*. That's an important spelling rule that you should know.

2-35. **box´es:** **Boxes** is the plural of box. That means there is *more than one box*.

-ly
(like, characteristics)
The ending –ly turns an adjective into an adverb.

2-36. **care´ful·ly:** Read the book **carefully** if you want to answer all the questions on the test. Take your time *and pay careful attention* to what you read.

2-37. **like´ly:** If you read carefully, it is **likely** that you will get a good grade on the test. You *probably* will do well if you read with care.

2-38. **re·li´a·bly:** If the mechanic does the work **reliably**, the car should run well for you for a long time. You *can rely on* a good mechanic to fix it right

2-39. **de·pen´da·bly:** I need my car to perform **dependably**. I want a dependable car that I *trust* to start and get me to work everyday

2-40. **a·bly:** Sam **ably** taught the history lesson to the students. He *was able* to teach them all about Abraham Lincoln and the Civil War.

2-41. **ca´pab·ly:** He **capably** fixed the dish washer so we could wash our dishes after supper. He was a very capable fixit man.

2-42. **o·be´di·ent·ly:** My German Shepherd dog **obediently** did what I asked him to do. He learned *to obey* at Dog Obedience School. He does what I tell him to do.

-ness
(state of)

2-43. **care´ful·ness: Carefulness** is important for a doctor performing surgery. You always want him to be careful all the time. **Carefulness** is the *state of being full of care.*

2-44. **blind´ness: Blindness** is a *state of being blind.* People with **blindness** are *unable to see.* They often need a trained Seeing Eye Dog to help them find their way.

2-45. **nice´ness:** People who practice **niceness** are great to be around. They are *nice to everyone* all the time. I hope you are nice to everyone.

2-46. **mean´ness: Meanness** is the *opposite of kindness.* Mean people are *not nice* to be around. Try to be nice to everyone, and you will have lots of good friends.

2-47. **kind´ness: Kindness** is a wonderful thing. We should be kind to everyone just as we want other people to be kind to us. Everyone is happier when we are *kind and caring.*

2-48. **la´zi·ness:** People who *refuse to work* suffer from a case of **laziness**. Lazy people never succeed in life. Lazy students often become lazy adults.

-able, -ible
(capable of, worthy, able to)

2-49. **ca´pa·ble:** Mark was a very **capable** farmer. He was *able* to grow the best crops and raise the healthiest animals.

2-50. **re·li´a·ble:** The tractor was very **reliable**. It *could be relied upon* to start every time and always pull the plow all day long.

2-51. **de·pend´a·ble:** Ron was very **dependable**. You could *depend on* him to do his homework everyday and never complain.

2-52. **de·fend´a·ble:** The army fort was very **defendable**. No matter how many soldiers the enemy sent to take the fort, the brave soldiers inside were *able to defend* it and keep the enemy from getting inside.

2-53. **de·fen´si·ble:** The soldiers took a **defensible** position behind some big rocks. They were *able to defend* their position and drive off the attackers.

2-54. **re·ver´si·ble:** Sharon bought a **reversible** jacket for her mother. Her mother could wear *either side out*. It was like having two jackets for the price of one.

2-55. **sen´si·ble:** My dad made a **sensible** decision when he bought our new car. It *made sense* that he bought a car that was very economical to drive and could hold everyone in our big family of twelve.

-ish
(related to)

2-56. **child´ish:** It is **childish** to squabble or argue over little things like who is going to be first in line. But sometimes even adults *act like children.*

2-57. **self´ish: Selfish** is *related to self.* **Selfish** people want everything for themselves and do not care for the needs or feelings of others. The opposite of **selfish** is generous.

2-58. **fool´ish:** It is **foolish** to think you can learn anything without studying. Wise students study hard and learn a lot. They are not **foolish.** A **foolish** person *lacks good sense or judgment.*

Chapter 3

Romance **Prefixes**

Romances (Latin/French) Elements of English
From the Golden Tongued Cicero
And the Mighty Roman Legions

Romance Prefixes
From Latin and French

Section 1

Long vowel sound
in open syllables
(vowel at the end of a syllable)

re-
(back, again)

3-1. **re·turn´:** The librarian said for us to **return** our library books before Thanksgiving vacation. We were *to turn them back in* before leaving.

3-2. **re·act´:** To **react** is how we act when something happens to us. How do you **react** when your mom asks you to make your bed? I hope you **react** happily without complaining.

3-3. **re·mem´ber:** It is good to **remember** the good things people do for us, and forget the bad. To **remember** is to *think about something again.*

3-4. **re·lax´:** Everyone needs to learn how to **relax.** To **relax** is to *take it easy* for a little while and think or do something relaxing. I play guitar to *relax.* What do you do?

3-5. **re·call´:** I cannot **recall** your telephone number. I cannot *remember* it. Please tell me again so I can memorize it.

3-6. **re·duce´:** The best way to **reduce** your weight is to balance your diet with exercise. A little less food and a little more exercises can help you to maintain a healthy weight.

de-
(from, away)

3-7. **de·form´:** The tree branches were very **deformed.** Its branches looked like scrawny, scary giant's fingers against the bright moonlight. They were *not normal.*

3-8. **de·part′:** The jet plane was going to **depart** at 4:30 in the morning. It was going to take off from the airport before the sun came up. To **depart** is *to leave.*

3-9. **de·light′:** The pie was a delicious **delight** to eat. It was a mouth watering pumpkin pie with whipped cream on top and a little cherry setting on the side. Yummy!

3-10. **de·part′ment:** My friend Jesse works in the watch **department**. He sells beautiful watches to the customers.

3-11. **de·stroy′:** The workmen had to **destroy** the old building because it was falling to pieces. It was dangerous and had to be torn down. They *put an end to it.*

3-12. **de·test′:** I delight in reading but **detest** math. I *do not like* math. I am lucky to have a good math tutor who makes sure that I learn how to work all the problems.

pre-
(before)

3-13. **pre-tend′:** Some boys and girls **pretend** that they are sick when they do not want to go to school. But they get well real quick and quit pretending to be sick when their mom says that she is going to take them to see the doctor for a shot. They were just *acting as if* they were sick.

3-14. **pre·view′:** **Preview** literally means to *view before.* We say we are going to **preview** a movie when we *see it before* it has come out in the movie theater.

3-15. **pre·vent′:** To **prevent** is *to keep something from happening.* An easy way to **prevent** an automobile accident is to watch were you are going and follow all the rules of the road.

bi-
(two)

3-16. **bi´cy·cle:** Mr. Potter loves to ride his tough Raleigh M-800 **bicycle** through the oil field trails of West Texas. The *bi* in bicycle means the **bicycle** has *two wheels*.

3-17. **bi·la´ter·al:** The two armies made a **bilateral** agreement to put down their arms and quit fighting. **Bilateral** means *two sides*. Both sides agreed to quit fighting.

3-18. **bi´fo·cals:** My grandpa wears **bifocals.** They are glasses with *two lenses*, one over the other, that help grandpa see things far away when he is driving his truck and up close when he is reading a book.

3-19. **bi·lin´gual:** Mr. Potter is **bilingual** because he speaks *two languages*. He can speak English and Spanish. Mr. Potter wants to teach everyone to speak and read English and Spanish because it is fun to know *two languages*.

tri-
(three)

3-20. **tri´an·gle:** A **triangle** has *three sides*. The Egyptians used **triangles** to design their pyramids.

3-21. **tri´cy·cle:** My cousin Laura has a new red **tricycle**. It is easier for her to ride than a bicycle because it has *three wheels*, making it easier to balance and not fall over.

3-22. **tri·lat´er·al:** France, Germany, and Spain made a **trilateral** agreement to not to fight anymore. **Trilateral** means *three sides*.

3-23. **tri·lin´gual**: María is **trilingual**. She can speak Hebrew, English and Spanish. She speaks *three languages*

pro-
(before, forward)

3-24. **pro·found´**: Einstein's discovery of the Theory of General Relativity made a **profound** difference in the way we look at the universe. A **profound** difference is a *big and important difference.*

3-25. **pro·duce´**: The Gibson Guitar Company can **produce** beautiful guitars that sound great. To **produce** is *to make or show.* Mr. Potter's favorite guitar is his Gibson ES-125.

3-26. **pro´ject**: The projector can **project** a picture on the screen in the front of the classroom. To verb **project** means to *throw something ahead.* The noun **project** is accented on the last syllable: pro·ject´ meaning *a plan.*

3-27. **pro·mote´**: Our librarian is trying to **promote** reading by buying some really exciting books for the library. To **promote** is *to support or actively encourage.* Mr. Potter is trying to **promote** the knowledge of Anglo Saxon and Latin prefixes with *Beyond Blend Phonics.*

co-
(together, with)

3-28. **co·or´di·nate**: The soldiers will **coordinate** their efforts in the night attack. They will make sure everyone is *working together* to accomplish the mission.

3-29. **co·ex·ist′: Coexist** means that two things *exist at the same time and same place*. When Mr. Potter was a kid, some farmers used horses and some used tractors. Farmers with tractors and farmers with horses **coexisted**.

3-30. **co·op′er·ate:** Boys on the basketball team **cooperate** to win the game. They *work together* to make the most baskets. We can accomplish a lot more when we **cooperate**.

Romance Prefixes
From Latin and French

Section 2

Short Vowels
in Closed Syllables
(Consonant at the End)

dis-
(separate, undoing)

3-31. **dis·like´:** Mr. Potter had a **dislike** for spinach when he was a little boy, but his good mother made him eat it anyway because it was good for him. Now he likes it a lot and eats some every week! When you **dislike** something you *do not like* it

3-32. **dis·place´:** Jim was **displaced** as the pitcher on his baseball team. Ron took over Jim's position on the baseball team while Jim's broken arm was healing. **Displace** means *to take over the place, position, or role of someone or something.*

3-33. **dis·play´:** Mr. Orson Potter, Donald Potter's dad, was a veteran of World War II. He liked to **display** the American Flag on a flagpole in his front yard to show his love for his country. He put it in a place where *everyone could see it.*

3-34. **dis·miss´:** Mrs. Green said she was going to **dismiss** the cheerleaders to go to the gym to prepare for the pep rally. She was going to *send them away* to the gym.

3-35. **dis·em·bark´:** The passengers were ready to **disembark** from the ship when it reached the dock. They were ready *to leave* the ship after suffering through the terrible hurricane.

3-36. **dis·cov´er:** It was a relief to **discover** that the pirate treasure was not at the bottom of the sea. It was *found* in the basement of the old house where it had been hidden over two-hundred years ago.

sub-
(under)

3-37. **sub´way:** We rode the **subway** to Central Park. The **subway** is a fast train that *runs under the ground.*

3-38. **sub·tract´:** Sandy learned to add and **subtract** in Mrs. Monroe's class. She learned that $5 - 2 = 3$. Her teacher called it *take away.*

3-39. **sub´ma·rine:** Oscar worked on a **submarine** that was studying the life of deep sea fish. His boat traveled *under the water* to extreme depths to where the deep sea fish live.

3-40. **sub·scribe´:** Mr. Potter wants to **subscribe** to a guitar magazine. He wants it to come to his house every month so he can practice new music on his Gibson ES-125 archtop electric guitar. To **subscribe** is *to arrange to receive something regularly.*

3-41. **sub·merge´:** A submarine has to be ready to **submerge** quickly if an enemy airplane is approaching. They have to be ready to *dive beneath* the water really fast to keep from being seen.

mis-
(wrong, bad)

3-42. **mis·place´:** If you are organized, you will not **misplace** your things. They will always be in the right place, and you will not have trouble finding them. To **misplace** is *to put something in the wrong place* and not be able to find it.

3-43. **mis·ap·ply´:** Have you ever accidentally put hand cream on your toothbrush? That is to **misapply** the hand cream and get a very bad taste in your mouth. **Misapply** means *to use something for the wrong purpose.*

3-44. **mis·un·der·stand´:** John speaks so softly that I often **misunderstand** him. I *can't understand* what he says.

3-45. **mis·in·for·ma´tion:** The boys gave us **misinformation** when they told us the game was at 5:30. It was at 5:00 instead. They gave us the *wrong information.*

in-
(in, not)

3-46. **in·a·bil´ity:** John's **inability** to understand new things kept him from buying a computer. John *lacked the ability* to learn new things so he didn't even try.

3-47. **in·ac´tive:** Gary's car was **inactive.** He parked it in the garage and quit driving it because it had a flat tire. It was *not in active use.* After fixing the tire, he put it back into active use.

3-48. **in·frc´queut:** Our visits to the big department store were **infrequent** because it was hard to find a place to park the car in the little parking lot. We *didn't go there very often.*

3-49. **in·ap·pro´pri·ate:** It is **inappropriate** to sing, whistle, or talk loudly in the library. It is *not appropriate* to makes these noises because they distract people who are trying to read. Libraries are supposed to be quiet so people can read in peace.

3-50. **in·com·plete´:** Sam's history homework is **incomplete**. He did *not complete* the essay about the Battle of Shiloh in the Civil War.

3-51. **in·cur´a·ble:** Jim's sister had an **incurable** disease. No one was able to cure it. It *couldn't be cured.*

3-52. **in·trans´i·tive:** An **intransitive** verb does not take a direct object. Transitive sentence: John hit the ball. **Intransitive** sentence: Jane ran fast.

im-
(in, not)

3-53. **im·pos´si·ble:** It is **impossible** to jump over a skyscraper. No one can do the **impossible** because it is *not possible.*

3-54. **im·pro´per:** It is **improper** to talk while you are eating. It is *not proper* to try to eat and speak at the same time.

3-55. **im·prac´ti·cal:** It is **impractical** to ride your bike to town in the pouring rain. It is *not practical* because you will be soaking wet by the time you get to town.

3-56. **im·pru´dent:** It is **imprudent** to spend more money than you make. It is *not a good idea* to spent lots of money and go deep in debt. An **imprudent** person makes *bad decisions.*

3-57. **im-pure´:** Never drink **impure** water because it might make you very sick. **Impure** water is water that is *not pure* because it has bad things in it that can make you sick.

ex-
(out)

3-58. **ex·pect′:** John memorized all his spelling words for the week. He was happy when he got an A+. You can **expect** to get an A+ if you study real hard.

3-59. **ex·port′:** Japan can **export** a lot of cars to America. They can *send out* a lot of cars. *Ex* means **out,** and *port* is the Latin root for **carry.** So **export** is literally, *"to carry out."*

3-60. **ex·tend′:** Mike was unable to **extend** his arm all the way after hurting it in a motorcycle accident. The doctor said that with physical therapy he will eventually be able to *move it all the way.*

3-61. **ex·press′:** Hanna was great at expressing her thoughts and feeling with words. She can **express** herself clearly on any subject. Everyone can understand her.

3-62. **ex·ter′mi·nate:** We called the exterminator to **exterminate** all the ants that had invaded our house. He was going to *kill* all of them with an insecticide.

trans-
(across)

3-63. **trans′late:** Mr. Potter likes to **translate** English to Spanish. He can tell Spanish speakers what an English speaker is saying. To **translate** is *to say in one language what someone said in another language.*

3-64. **trans´port:** They had to **transport** the sick boy to another hospital in a helicopter because it was the fastest way. **Transport** means *to take people or things from one place to another.* **Port** is the Latin word for *carry.*

3-65. **trans´form:** A poor student can **transform** himself or herself into a good student by hard work and study. To **transform** is to make a thorough or dramatic *change in form.*

3-66. **trans·mis´sion:** The electric **transmission** lines carry electricity all across the country. The electricity is transmitted or *carried* through lines from the power company to the houses, schools, and businesses.

non-
(not)

3-67. **non´sense:** Ricky told his little sister that it was **nonsense** to be scared of little green men under her bed. She asked what **nonsense** meant. He replied, "It *doesn't make any sense* to believe in little green men hiding under the bed at night.

3-68. **non·des·cript´:** The Porter family lived in a **nondescript** house on the south side of town. They lived in a house that looked like all the other houses on that side town. You couldn't tell one house from the other.

3-69. **non·ad·dic´tive:** They say that aspirin is **nonaddictive.** You will *not get addicted* to it if you take it for a headache or to alleviate pain. An **addictive** drug is *hard to quit taking* once you get hooked on it.

3-70. **non·con·duc´tive:** A **nonconductive** metal will *not conduct* electricity. You can connect it to all the batteries you want, and it still will *not let electricity flow* through it.

3-71. **non·a·ligned´:** The tires on the old car were **nonaligned**. They were *not lined up* to track correctly, and that made the car pull to the left and to be hard to steer. We need to take them to an alignment shop and get them aligned so the car will drive straight and be easy to steer.

3-72. **non·prof´it:** My dad owns a **nonprofit** company. His company *does not make a profit*. It just gives away Mr. Potter's phonics books to help more people learn how to read.

uni-
(one)

3-73. **un´i·form:** The nurses all wear green **uniforms.** They all look alike. They have just *one form* so they are called **uniforms**!

3-74. **u´ni·corn:** My sister Kelly got a toy **unicorn**. It is a cuddly little stuffed horse with a *single horn* on its forehead.

3-75. **u·ni·la´ter·al:** Our government made a **unilateral** decision not to enter into the trade agreement. We made the decision on our own. The decision was *one sided*. We did not consult anybody else to see what they thought.

3-76. **u´ni·cy·cle:** Roger got a **unicycle** for his birthday. It is a bicycle with only *one wheel*. It took him a long time to learn how to ride it without falling over

mal-
(bad, evil)

3-77. **mal·nu·tri´tion:** The baby was suffering from **malnutrition**. He was *not getting proper nutrition.* He was not getting the nutritious food he needed to be healthy.

3-78. **mal·con·tent´:** The factory workers were **malcontent** with their wages. They were *not happy* with the money they earned everyday. They thought they needed more money.

3-79. **mal·func´tion:** The red sports car had a **malfunction** on the road. The hose from the gas tank sprang a leak so the car stopped running. It *quit functioning properly.*

3-80. **mal·nour´ished:** I could tell that the skinny dog was **malnourished**. His owner did not feed him the right kind of dog food. The dog needed food that was more nourishing so he could put on some weight and get healthy.

bene-
(well, good)

3-81. **ben´e·fit:** They had a **benefit** to get money to buy warm clothes for one of the needy students. **To benefit** means *to help.* The warm clothes would *help* them stay warm during the cold winter weather.

3-82. **be·ne·fac´tor:** The school found a **benefactor** who gave them over $100,000 to build new classrooms. A **benefactor** is a person who gives money *to help a person or cause.*

3-83. **be·ne·dic´tion:** John gave a good **benediction** at the end of the wedding. A **benediction** is *a prayer at the end of a service.*

inter-
(among, between)

3-84. **in·ter·ac´tion:** The Rising Sun basketball team had great **interaction** this evening in the game. They all *acted together* to win the game. Way to go Shiners!

3-85. **in·ter´state:** The **Interstate** Highway System allows us to get *from one state to another state* in America really fast. **Interstate** Twenty is an **Interstate** highway that crosses several states.

3-86. **in·ter·act´:** The counselor noted that the kids are **interacting** well now that they have solved their problems. They *play and work together* without fighting and are having lots of fun together.

3-87. **in·ter·vene´:** The referee had to **intervene** when the football players started getting upset with each other. The referee *stepped in* and stopped the fight. He was a good referee.

3-88. **in·ter·rupt´:** It is not nice to **interrupt** adults when they are talking. You should *not bother* adults when they are talking.

3-89. **in·ter-change´:** The **interchange** of stories was a great idea. The kids got together everyday *to share* and *swap* stories.

3-90. **in·ter·face′**: The computer could not **interface** with the printer. I could not get them *connected to each other.*

3-91. **in·ter·ject′**: Harvey was able to **interject** a good idea into our discussion about how to train a bird dog to hunt. He *inserted* a good idea into our discussion about teaching the dog to chase the bird.

intra-
(within, inside)

3-92. **in·tra·a·to′mic**: The physicists are looking for more **intraatomic** particles: the little pieces of matter that make up the tiny *inner parts of the atom.*

3-93. **in·tra·state′**: The **intrastate** highway runs *inside a state* and not between states. The states build and maintain **intrastate** highways.

intro-
(into, inward)

3-94. **in·tro·duce′**: Let me **introduce** you to my best friend, Rodger. He lives just down the street from my house. He loves to play chess. To **introduce** is *to make someone known by name for the first time.*

3-95. **in·tro·duc′tion**: The **introduction** of the book was so interesting that I had to read the whole book. An **introduction** tells you *what the book is about.*

3-96. **in·tro·vert′**: I think Sharon is an **introvert** because she seems to prefer to be by herself. Maybe she is just *shy.* Let's see if we can get to be friends with her.

post-
(after, behind)

3-97. **post´date:** My student asked me to **postdate** the check until she was able to put money in the bank to cover it. She wrote a *future date* on the check when she would have money in the bank to pay me. I should not cash it before that date because the money will not be there till then.

3-98. **post´haste:** We should go to the class **posthaste**. We should go to the class *right now!* **Posthaste** means very *quickly* or *immediately*.

3-99. **post·grad´u·ate:** Mr. Potter would like to do **postgraduate** studies in the Science of Reading. He would like to do advanced university level work in how children learn to read.

3-100. **post·pone´:** The Cardinals had to **postpone** the baseball game because of rain. They were going to *put off* the game because of rain and *play it later* when the rain was over. To **postpone** *is to arrange for something to happen later than first scheduled.*

Romance Prefixes From Latin and French

Section 3

Disguised Prefixes

Note the double consonants that often occur. Prefixes ending in *-l* come before a root beginning with *l*; *r* before *r*; and *m* before *m*, *b*, and *p*. etc.

Disguised prefixes are sometimes called **Chameleon prefixes** because they change their form just like chameleons change their color to blend in with their surroundings. Linguists call this change of form, **assimilation**.

con- [col-, com-, cor-]
(together, with)

3-101. **con·fide´:** Mary thought she could **confide** in Sally and trust her not to tell her deepest secret to anyone. Sally would never tell anyone. To **confide** *is to tell someone a secret while trusting them not to repeat it to others.*

3-102. **con·ver·sa´tion:** It is fun to have a **conversation** with a friend who likes the same things as you like. You can *talk* to them about riding motorcycles, fishing, playing baseball and football, strumming guitars, and your favorite poems and novels.

3-103. **con·clu´sion:** Scientists came to the **conclusion** that some diseases are caused by germs. They looked at germs in a microscope and *decided* that they caused the sickness.

3-104. **con·junc´tion:** In English class we learn that **conjunctions** are an important part of speech. Some important **conjunctions** to know are: *and, or, but*, and *nor.* They *join* words, phrases, and sentences.

3-105. **con´vict:** The man had been a **convict** and had spent ten years in prison. He was convicted for selling drugs. A counselor helped when he got out so he never sold any more drugs. (**Con·vict´** means to *prove guilty.*)

3-106. **con·vince´:** Judy wanted to **convince** her brother that she was taller than him, so she got a ruler and measured them both. He was *persuaded* when he saw the evidence.

3-107. **con·nect′:** You have to **connect** the cables to the speakers if you want to hear the music. To **connect** is to *hook things together.*

3-108. **con·clude′:** We can **conclude** that the book is really good once we finish reading it. There is no way *to decide* if the book is good or not until we have read it.

3-109. **col·lect′:** Martha likes to **collect** coins. She has collected a lot of them in a coin book. To **collect** is to *bring or gather together.*

3-110. **col·lide′:** Mark and William were about to **collide** into each other when playing basketball. They almost *ran into each other* because they were not looking where they were going. They stopped just in time and prevented a collision.

3-111. **col·li′sion:** Junior and Frank's cars had a **collision** when Junior failed to stop at the stop sign. They *crashed.* Fortunately, no one was hurt. Junior will be more careful the next time he drives.

3-112. **col·lu′sion:** The teacher knew there was **collusion** when both boys turned in identical answers on their tests. They *got together to cheat.* Fortunately she caught them and put a stop to their **collusion.**

3-113. **com-part′ment:** I keep a flashlight in the glove **compartment** of my car. A **compartment** is a *little place to store things.*

3-114. **com′pound:** *Hotdog* and *steamship* are **compound** words. They are made of two different words put together to make a new word.

3-115. **com·mu′ni·cate:** In school, we learn to **communicate** with others in writing by studying phonics, spelling, and rhetoric. It is important to learn *to share our feelings and ideas* clearly so we can be understood.

3-116. **com·bine′:** The basketball team members **combine** their talents to make a great team. They *put together* their skills such as dribbling, passing, shooting, and blocking to win the game.

3-117. **cor·rect′:** The teacher asked Sandy to **correct** the mistakes in her composition. It was a good composition, but she needed to *make corrections* in the spelling. She *fixed* her all the misspelled words.

3-118. **cor·rode′:** If you leave your bicycle out in the rain, it will **corrode.** It will *get rusty* and become very hard to ride.

3-119. **cor·ro′sion:** The result of leaving your bicycle in the rain is **corrosion. Corrosion** is the *rust* that gets on the chain that makes it hard to peddle your bike. Oil your bike often to keep it free from **corrosion.**

in- [im-, ir-]
(in, into)

3-120. **in·vite′:** I decided to **invite** all my school friends to my birthday party. I am writing letters of invitation *to ask them to come* and enjoy the fun of jumping on a great big jumper in my backyard.

3-121. **in·vent´:** Thomas Edison was able to **invent** the electric light bulb by trying many different materials until he found the right one. He was the one of the greatest inventors of all times. To **invent** is *to create or make something new.*

3-122. **in·crease´:** You can **increase** your grades by studying hard and turning in all your homework on time. You can *raise* your grades by doing your work the best you can.

3-123. **in·tend´:** Do you **intend** to go to my birthday party? I hope you *plan* to attend. It is going to be lots of fun.

3-124. **im·port´:** Dad's new car is an **import.** It was made in Germany. They **import** good cars from Germany. **Import** means to *bring in.*

3-125. **im·mor´tal:** A person who is **immortal** will *never die.* A person who is **immortal** is said to have immortality.

3-126. **im·bibe´: Imbibe** means *to drink.* It usually refers to a drink with alcohol in it. Mr. Potter does not drink alcohol. He recommends that all his students never drink alcohol since it causes a lot of problems for a lot of people.

3-127. **im·bal´ance:** Some people have an eating **imbalance.** They either eat too much or too little. You should have a good balance of all the food from all the food groups to be healthy.

3-128. **im·por´tant:** Reading is a very **important** subject. Crystal's parents know that reading is *valuable.* That is why they take her to the library every week to check out new books to read.

3-129. **im·pound′:** When the police **impound** a car, they take it to a special locked parking lot. The owner cannot get it till he pays his fine and gets permission to pick up his car.

3-130. **ir·reg′u·lar:** Jack missed a lot of school. He was very **irregular** in his attendance. He was *not regular* in his attendance. He showed up whenever he wanted to.

3-131. **ir′ri·tate:** Willie can really **irritate** his teacher by constantly tapping his pencil on the table. His tapping *bothers* his teacher a lot. It **irritates** her terribly.

3-132. **ir·res·pon′si·ble:** Harry is very **irresponsible.** He forgot his homework three times this week. He is *not responsible*. He needs a lesson in responsibility.

3-133. **ir′ri·gate:** Dad has to **irrigate** the front yard three time a week. He *waters* the front yard three time a week so we can have a nice green yard. Irrigation keeps the yard green.

3-134. **ir·res·pon′sive:** The television was **irresponsive** to the controller. It did *not respond* because the batteries had run out. The television was responsive again once we put fresh batteries in the controller.

3-135. **ir·ri·ga′tion: Irrigation** is the only way that cotton farmers in West Texas are able to grow cotton. It almost never rains so they have to irrigate. To irrigate means *to water*.

sub- [suc-, suf-, sug-]
(under)

3-136. **sub·tract´**: **Subtract** means *to take away*. Two minus one is a subtraction problem. The answer, of course, is one. Learn to add fast, and subtraction will be easy.

3-137. **sub´ma·rine**: The **submarine** could stay under the water for weeks at a time. A **submarine** is a boat that travels *under the water*.

3-138. **sub´ject**: The **subject** of a sentence is what the sentence is about. The sentence, "John ate the apple." is all about John. John is the **subject**. What is the **subject** of the next sentence? Spelling can be hard. Hint, "What can be hard?"

3-139 **sub-jec´tive**: His opinion on the best car to buy is very **subjective**. It is just his own *opinion*.

3-140. **sub·scribe´**: Mr. Potter likes to **subscribe** to <u>Popular Science</u>. He *pays for it to be delivered* to his house every month. He got a subscription from his granddaughter.

3-141. **sub´way**: Do you like to ride the **subway** to work? The **subway** is a *train that runs under the ground*.

3-142. **sub´ju·gate**: Some settlers wanted to **subjugate** the natives and make them slaves. They wanted to *conquer* and *control* them.

3-143. **suc·ceed´**: To **succeed** you have to work hard and prepare yourself to capture the moment. To **succeed** is the opposite of to fail. To **succeed** is *to achieve a desired aim or result*.

3-144. **suc·cess´:** You can be a **success** if you apply yourself. **Success** is the opposite of failure. **Success** is *being able to reach an aim or purpose.*

3-145. **suf·fix´:** We are studying **suffixes** of Latin origin. Learn the meaning of a **suffix**, and you can read a lot of words. The **suffixes** carry meaning and are attached (affixed) to the *ends* of words.

3-146. **suf´fer:** My uncle **suffers** a lot from pain in his back. To **suffer** means to *hurt* and *feel bad*.

3-147. **suf·fi´cient:** Do we have **sufficient** milk to last the whole week? Do we have *enough* milk to last the whole week?

3-148. **sug·gest´:** Where do you **suggest** that we go to eat this evening? I **suggest** that we eat at a good restaurant. That is my *recommendation*.

3-149. **sug·ges´tive:** Mary is very **suggestive**. She didn't actually say she wanted to eat a hamburger. She just **suggested** it when she said, "Why don't we eat at Margie's Diner tonight." She *hinted*.

ad- [ac, af, ag, al, ap, af, as, at]
(to, toward)

3-150. **ad´dress:** Harvey Miller's **address** is 1275 April St., Appleton, Idaho. That is *where he lives*. His mail is delivered to that location.

3-151. **ad´dict:** An **addict** is *a person addicted to a drug*. I hope you never get addicted to any harmful drug because addiction can destroy your life. It can be hard to quit.

3-152 **ad·dic´ted: Addicted** means that the person is so *dependent* on a particular substance or drug that they are unable to quite taking it without feeling very bad.

3-153. **af·ford´:** Can we **afford** to eat at the nice new restaurant on Central Street? I hear it is very expensive. Do we *have enough money* for the expensive meal?

3-154. **af·fix´: Affix** is another word for *attach*. You can **affix** a stamp to an envelope by wetting the back and *gluing* it to the envelope.

3-155. **al·lot´: Allot** means *to share something*. I was **allotted** a little room in the back of the house. They *gave* me a little room to sleep in. It was my allotment.

3-156. **al·low´ance:** Johnny's father told him that he was going to give him an **allowance**. Everyday Johnny was to make his bed, take out the trash, cut wood for the fireplace, feed the cows and calves, give the horse grain, and milk two cows. He got a dollar a week for doing his chores. Do you get an **allowance**? How much?

3-157. **al·le´vi·ate:** Sometimes when I get a bad headache, I will take an aspirin to **alleviate** the pain. **Alleviate** means to *reduce pain and suffering*.

3-158. **ac·count´:** Henry put some of his allowance in a bank **account** instead of spending it all. That way he was able to save up money for important things later like an education. The bank keeps his money for him. The bank can **account** for his money because they know exactly where it is and how much there is.

3-159. **ac·cord′:** Johnny's teacher and parents were in **accord** that Johnny should stay in at recess and do his homework. They *agreed* that he should stay in and do the work that he failed to do at home.

3-160. **ac·cept′:** My dad was glad to **accept** a new job at the factory. He *agreed to take* the job because they promised to give him a lot more money.

3-161. **ac′ci·dent:** Mary had an **accident** in the classroom. She accidentally spilled purple soft drink on the floor. She *didn't do it on purpose*. It was an **accident**. The teacher was able to clean it up with water.

3-162. **ag·gres′sive:** Jean made an **aggressive** attempt to learn all her spelling words. She attacked every word on the hard list, studying it until she knew it perfectly. She got a good grade because she *got serious* about studying.

3-163. **ag′gra·vate′:** Mom's car used to **aggravate** her when it wouldn't start on cold mornings. She took it to the shop and got a new battery. Now her car starts in the coldest weather, and she isn't *bothered* any more. To **aggravate** is *to bother*.

3-164. **ap·proach′:** Jim heard the bear **approach** him in the still darkness. He could tell that it was *coming nearer* and nearer as the twigs snapped and the leaves rustled. He grabbed his trusty rifle and turned on his light. To his relief, it was just his little brother eating a midnight snack!

3-165. **ap·point′:** They decided to **appoint** Howard's dad to coach the basketball team until the coach got back from vacation. Howard's dad was *assigned* the job of coaching for awhile.

3-166. **ap·pear´:** The children in the bus accident did not **appear** to be hurt. They did not *look like* they were injured, but they went to the doctor just to make sure. The doctor said everyone was fine and could go home.

3-167. **ap·por´tion:** The teacher decided to **apportion** the snacks to the students fairly. She *divided* the pretzels evenly *between* the students so everyone got exactly the same number of delicious pretzels. She was being fair to everyone.

3-168. **ar·ri´val:** The **arrival** of the new student was welcomed by all. She came all the way from Columbia. Mr. Potter welcomed her in Spanish. Arrival is *the act of arriving.*

3-169. **ar·range´:** Mr. Potter likes the way his grandson **arranges** his toys in his room. Everything is well organized and easy to find.

3-170. **as·sign´:** Mrs. Pearl Monroe said she was going to **assign** Clayton to sharpen the pencils and clean the chalkboard everyday for the whole week. She *made it his job* to do those things. He was happy to be her helper.

3-171. **as·sem´ble:** Mom and Dad had to **assemble** the new computer desk. They had to *put it together.*

3-172. **as·sort´:** **Assort** is an archaic word (very old word not used much anymore) for *classify.* Dad bought an **assortment** of candy. It contained several *different kinds* of candy.

3-173. **as·sort´ment:** Dad had a big **assortment** of nuts and bolts. He could usually find what he needed because he had so many different sizes of nuts and bolts. He had a very large *collection.*

3-174. **at·tack´:** The army closed in for the **attack**. They had everything ready to *take the action to defeat the enemy.*

3-175. **at·tend´:** Mr. Potter's grandkids **attend** a private school, where they get a great education. They *go to* a school that still teaches sentence diagramming and cursive handwriting. It's a great school!

3-176. **at·ten´tion:** To learn anything, you have to pay **attention**. Johnny *listens carefully* in American History. He can name all the presidents of the United States.

3-177. **at·tract´:** We learned that a magnet can **attract** certain kinds of metal. The magnet *pulls* the metal to it. Kids love to play with magnets.

3-178. **at-trac´tion:** The log cutting was the major **attraction** at this year's fair. It attracted a lot of people to the fair to see the lumberjacks cut logs by hand with an ax and crosscut saw. An **attraction** is *something that attracts people.*

Chapter 4

Romance **Suffixes**

Romances (Latin/French) Elements of English
From the Golden Tongued Cicero
And the Mighty Roman Legions

-ist
(noun, person)

4-1. **den′tist:** I have a wonderful **dentist**. He knows how to keep my teeth clean and healthy.

4-2. **sci′en·tist:** To be a **scientist**, you have to know a lot about math and experimental methods. **Scientists** *discover the truth about nature through experiments.*

4-3. **chem′ist:** A **chemist** is *a person who experiments to find out how materials interact.* The oil company employs a lot of **chemists** to help make the best oils for our cars.

4-4. **flu′tist:** Joan is a **flutist** in the school concert orchestra. She *plays a flute* in the orchestra.

4-5. **gui·tar′ist:** Mr. Potter is a **guitarist.** His favorite guitar is a Gibson ES-125 archtop electric that he bought in 1964 at the Lambert Music Store in Cincinnati, Ohio. He *plays guitar* everyday.

4-6. **vi·o·lin′ist:** Mr. Potter's daughter was a **violinist** in the orchestra. She played beautiful music on her violin.

4-7. **art′ist:** Rembrandt was a great Flemish **artist**. His beautiful art work is in some of the best museums in the world. An **artist** *makes paintings and drawings.*

-ive
(tending to, having the nature of)

4-8. **act′ive:** Devin is an **active** little boy. He can't sit still for more than ten minutes. He always has to be doing something. He is very **active**.

4-9. **ad·dic´tive:** Nicotine in cigarettes is very **addictive**. It is *habit forming*, making it very hard to quit smoking once you start. It is better never to start smoking.

4-10. **ag·gress´ive:** The dog was so **aggressive** that his owner had to keep him on a chain all the time. He was *mean and dangerous*. If he got loose, he might bite someone.

4-11. **co·hes´ive:** The basketball team was very **cohesive**. They *stuck together* and *worked together* well to win a lot of games.

4-12. **as·ser´tive:** John was very **assertive**. He always says what he wants and manages to have his way. He asserts himself.

4-13. **di·ges´tive:** The **digestive** tract is where our food is digested. The food is *broken down* in the digestive tract so it can be used by the body for energy and growth.

4-14. **rel´a·tive:** George is a **relative** of mine. He is my cousin. His dad and my dad are twin brothers.

4-15. **sen´si·tive:** Mary is very **sensitive** about her black eye. She doesn't want anyone to see it. She had a bad fall out of a tree. She will be well soon. She I *easily offended*.

-age
(belonging to, relating to)

4-16. **cour´age:** Charles Lindbergh had a lot of **courage** to fly across the Atlantic Ocean by himself in a little single engine plane. He was very *brave and fearless*.

4-17. **sal´vage:** We went down to the **salvage** yard to get a part for Dad's car. A **salvage** yard is where they take parts off old cars to use them again. They *rescue* the parts.

4-18. **stor´age:** We have a **storage** shed in the backyard. We *store* things we need for yard work in our shed.

4-19. **for´age:** Squirrels have to **forage** for nuts in the winter. They have to *search widely* for them.

4-20. **man´age:** Everyone needs to learn how to **manage** their money. They need to learn how to *control* their spending so they don't spend more than they make.

4-21. **pill´age:** The Vikings used to **pillage** the towns along the coast of England. They used to go in and *take anything they wanted by violence during the wars.*

4-22. **mar´riage:** Mr. Potter tells us that a **marriage** is supposed to last for lifetime. Married people love each other and live together always. **Marriage** is between a man and a woman.

-ant
(full of)

4-23. **a·bund´ant:** The party had **abundant** refreshments. They had *plenty* of refreshments for everyone.

4-24. **de·fend´ant:** Margaret was a **defendant** in a court case. She had to defend herself against a charge that she had been driving too fast.

4-25. **el´e·gant:** Martha had a very **elegant** new watch. It was made of gold and had four diamonds. It was very *fancy*.

4-26. **en´trant:** Billy was an **entrant** in the relay race at the high school. He had signed up *to enter* the race.

4-27. **ob·serv´ant:** Laura was very **observant**. She *paid good attention* in class and learned a lot. She never missed anything the teacher taught.

4-28. **ten´ant:** Joseph was a **tenant** in an apartment building. He lived in an apartment building that *he rented from his landlord*, Mr. Thomas.

4-29. **de·fi´ant:** Karen was **defiant**. She was determined not to eat spinach. But her mother asked her to try some. She did. Now she is compliant, and not **defiant**.

4-30. **brilli´ant:** Learning Latin suffixes will make people think your are **brilliant**. They will think you are *real smart* because you can read advanced English words from Latin.

-ent
(full of)

4-31. **co·her´ent:** John's argument for learning Latin suffixes was **coherent**. His argument *made a lot of sense*. They helped him expand his vocabulary and read richer literature.

4-32. **ab´sent:** William is **absent** today. His mom called in to say that he was sick and would not make it to school. He *will not be there*.

4-33. de·pend´ent: Babies are completely **dependent** on their parents to feed, clothe, teach, and love them. They depend on them. The root *pend* means *to hang,* and little kids love to hang onto their mothers.

4-34. com´pe·tent: Ricky is **competent** to take the test. He studied hard and knows all the answers. He will get a good grade. He *has the necessary ability, knowledge, and skills to be successful.*

4-35. em´i·nent: John Williams is an **eminent** classical guitar player. He is *very well known* as being one of the best players of classical guitar music. He can play Bach really well.

4-36. res´i·dent: Mr. Potter is a **resident** of Odessa, Texas. He *resides* or *lives in* Odessa, Texas.

4-37. flu´ent: Mr. Potter works hard to teach his students to be **fluent** in speaking Spanish. He wants them to *speak it very well.*

4-38. in·de·pend´ent: Jean is very **independent** at school. She does *not depend* on anyone. She does all her work herself.

-or
(a person who)

4-39. ac´tor: Jackson is going to be an **actor** in the school play. He is going to play the part of a funny clown. He can *act* well. An **actor** is *a person who acts.*

4-40. doc´tor: My **doctor** said that with a little rest I would be as good as new. A **doctor** is *someone who practices medicine and helps sick people get well.*

4-41. **ed´i·tor:** The **editor** of books is responsible to make sure the books are ready for publication. He *edits* or *checks* the books for grammar, spelling, style, and content.

4-42. **col·lec´tor:** Sam was a **collector** of butterflies. He had a large collection of butterflies. They were all neatly arranged on a board for viewing. A **collector** *collects things.*

4-43. **in·ven´tor:** Thomas Edison was one of the greatest **inventors** that ever lived. He invented the incandescent light bulb, phonograph record player, and many other useful things. Inventors *make new things.*

4-44. **pro·fes´sor: Professor** George González was one of Mr. Potter's favorite **professors.** He taught Mr. Potter how to write sentences to teach the meaning of new words like **professor!** A **professor** is *a respected teacher in a college or university.*

4-45. **tran·sla´tor:** Mr. Potter teaches his student how to **translate** between English and Spanish. His students are learning to translate. A **translator** can tell you what someone says in the another language.

-ar
(adjective)

4-46. **an´gu·lar:** The modern painter, Pablo Picasso's, pictures showed **angular** shapes. His pictures used *angles* to represent objects and people.

4-47. **pop´u·lar:** Mary is a very **popular** student at school. *Everybody likes her* because she is so nice and helpful.

4-48. **mus´cu·lar:** Jim is a **muscular** gymnast. He has lots of *strong muscles* and is able to do lot of tricks on the high bar.

4-49. **cir´cu·lar:** In drivers' training class, Mark drove the car in a **circular** motion, *round and round* the school parking lot to learn to steer and control the car.

4-50. **so´lar:** We cooked hotdogs on a **solar** cooker. It is a device that gets hot enough in the *sun* to cook hotdogs

4-51. **lu´nar:** Mr. Potter was a college student when the **Lunar** Lander landed the first men on the moon. **Lunar** is an adjective referring to the *moon.*

-ible
(can be done)

4-52. **ed´i·ble:** An apple is **edible**. It is safe and good to eat. Literally, *able to be eaten.*

4-53. **in·cred´i·ble:** John told us an **incredible** story about a boy who tamed a dinosaur. It was *not* a *credible* or *believable* story. **Cred** in **incredible** means *believe,* **in** means *not.*

4-54. **hor´ri·ble:** Sam had a **horrible** cold. His cold was very terrible. He felt *very bad* for a long time.

4-55. **im·pos´si·ble:** It is **impossible** for a cow to jump over the moon in the real world. It is *not possible* for cows to jump that far. But in nursery rhymes, they can do it easily.

4-56. **au´di·ble:** **Audible** books are now available at the bookstore. They are books on cassette or CD's that you can *listen* to instead of having to read yourself.

4-57. **ter´ri·ble:** Robert had a **terrible** cough. He started coughing and couldn't stop. It was *really horrible.*

4-58. **for´ci·ble:** The police made a **forcible** entry into the house. The man inside wouldn't let them in so they had to knock down the door and *force* their way in.

-ary
(connecting with, adjective or noun)

4-59. **san´i·tar·y:** Hospitals are very **sanitary**. The make sure everything is *really clean* and *free of germs.*

4-60. **mil´i·tar·y:** America has a strong **military.** They have very good soldiers, excellent commanders, and the finest military equipment.

4-61. **pri´mar·y:** Mr. Potter's **primary** goal is to teach all his students to read well and think clearly. It is his *main and most important* goal.

4-62. **dic´tion·ar·y:** Kim uses her **dictionary** all the time to learn new words. A **dictionary** tells us the spelling, meaning, and pronunciation of words. The suffix –ary forms a noun.

-ize
(to make or put to)

4-63. **re´a·lize:** I did not **realize** that reading could be so much fun until Mr. Potter suggested that I read <u>The Bears of Blue River</u>. What an exciting book written in 1900!

4-64. **pas´teur·ize:** They **pasteurize** milk by *heating it to kill all the bad bacteria* that can makes us sick. I always drink **pasteurized** milk.

4-65. **mo´der·nize:** Last week my teacher decided to **modernize** our classroom by buying a computer with learning games installed. Now her classroom is *modern* and *up-to-date.* The best game was <u>Read, Write, and Type.</u>

4-66. **mem´or·ize:** Mrs. Monroe showed us how to **memorize** poems. By repetition and concentration, we *store them in our memory* so we can recite them later.

-ar
(noun)

4-67. **doll´ar:** Mom gave me a **dollar** to buy candy at the store. A **dollar** is *one-hundred pennies.*

4-68. **li´ar:** Our teacher told us that a **liar** would always get into trouble. It is always better to tell the truth. A **liar** is someone who *does not tell the truth.*

4-69. **pill´ar:** There were four **pillars** holding up the porch. The **pillars** hold up the roof.

-ance
(state of)

4-70. **as·sur´ance:** Our teacher gave us her **assurance** that if we did all our work in biology we would learn a lot about plants and animals. She *made us believe* that if we completed our assignments we would master the subject.

4-71. **coun´ten·ance:** Frank's **countenance** brightened up, and he smiled when he learned that he got a perfect score on the hard spelling test. He had a *smile on his face.*

4-72. **re·li´ance:** We had **reliance** in our car's ability to start every time. We *rely* on it to start and get us to our destination. We *trust* it to perform reliably.

-(t)ure
(noun showing action, condition, process, function)

4-73. **pas´ture:** The cows eat grass in the **pasture**. The cows graze on green grass in the **pasture** and convert it into delicious milk. **Pasture** is *land covered with grass*.

4-74. **lec´ture:** Last week a visiting professor gave a wonderful **lecture** on the mysteries of Quantum Physics. He gave an *educational talk* to our school.

4-75. **fu´ture:** It is impossible to completely know the **future**. The past is behind us. The present is with us. The **future** is before us. It *hasn't happened yet*.

4-76. **de·par´ture:** Tim and Mary's **departure** time is ten o'clock in the morning. They will be *leaving* on the jetliner at 10:00 a.m.

4-77. **ad·ven´ture:** Mr. Potter thinks the *Iliad* by Homer is the oldest and greatest **adventure** story of all time. He suggested that we read it in a modern version.

4-78. **ex·pen´di·ture:** The principal told the teachers that they would have to cut **expenditures** for the rest of the year. They would have to reduce their *expenses* and not spend so much money.

4-79. **fix´ture:** They bought a new light **fixture** for the room so they can see better. A **fixture** is a piece of furniture fixed in one position so it *can not move.*

-tion, -sion
(Forming nouns of action, state of being, result, or condition)

> Note: The vowel digraph (io) is pronounced as a schwa sound /ŭ/. The initial consonants are all pronounced like /sh/ as in <u>shoe</u>. The consonants, *c, t,* and *s* are often part of the root word.

4-80. **va·ca´tion:** We went to the mountains to go snow skiing during the winter **vacation.** Spring **vacation** is almost here. A **vacation** is *an extended period of recreation.*

4-81. **dis·trac´tion:** Our teacher says that whistling during a reading lesson is a **distraction.** It *distracts* or draws our attention away from what the teacher is teaching us.

4-82. **sub·trac´tion: Subtraction** is *an arithmetical operation of taking a smaller number away from a larger number.* **Subtraction** is easy if you know how to add.

4-83. **ad·di´tion: Addition** is one of the first things that we learn in arithmetic. Three apples plus four apples is seven apples. That's a simple **addition** problem. $4 + 7 = 11$.

4-84. **di·rec´tion:** Follow the teacher's **direction** if you want to do the work correctly. Learning to follow **directions** is one of the most important things we learn in school.

4-85. **ex·pe·di´tion:** Richard E. Byrd lead several **expeditions** to the Antarctic. He was a very brave explorer to make these *adventurous trips.*

4-86. nu·tri′tion: An apple is one of the best foods for good **nutrition** An apple has lots of vitamins and minerals that make it nutritious and *good for our health.*

4-87. re·pe·ti′tion: Mrs. Monroe told us that **repetition** was the Mother of Learning. By that she meant that the more we *repeat* what we want to learn the better we learn it. To repeat is *to say or do again.*

4-88. par·ti′tion: The one-room school house had a **partition** between the first and second grades. They put up a curtain between the classes so each class could have some privacy.

4-89. i·ni·ti·a′tion: Rodger had to memorize and recite three of Robert Browning's poems before he could become a member of the *Browning Poetry Society.* It was part of the **initiation** into the club before he could *become a member.*

4-90. no·ti·fi·ca′tion: They sent our parents a **notification** that our third-grade class would be having a Thanksgiving program next Saturday. They sent our parents a *note* to let them know.

4-91. de·ten′tion: Poor Ralph had **detention** at lunch. He had to *stay in* and eat by himself during lunch because he had broken a rule.

-sion
(Forming nouns of action, state of being, result, or condition)

The suffix –sion can have two pronunciation:
1. After a vowel or consonant r it is pronounced /zhŭn/.
2. After any consonant except r it is pronounced /shŭn/.

4-92. **in·va′sion:** On June 6, 1944 the Allies launched the greatest **invasion** for freedom in the history of mankind. They stormed the well fortified beaches of Normandy to gain a great victory for human freedom and dignity.

4-93. **con·clu′sion:** Do not draw a **conclusion** until you have enough facts to make a good decision. Making a decision without all the facts is called a "hasty **conclusion**." A hasty **conclusion** can lead to a bad decision. A **conclusion** is *a judgment reached by reason.*

4-94. **ex·clu′sion:** Harry failed to read the **exclusion** clause in the contact for the apartment. It said that pets were *excluded.* They were *not allowed* in the apartments.

4-95. **e·va′sion:** Jim's answer was actually an **evasion**. Instead of answering the question, he started talking about something else *to avoid having to answer* the question.

4-96. **a·ver′sion:** Shawn had an **aversion** to doing math problems. He *didn't like* doing the problems and didn't want to do them. He said it make him sick. A good tutor can help him learn to like math.

4-97. **con·ver′sion:** Students in America today have to learn the **conversion** of metric units to standard English units. They have to learn to *convert* or *change* them from one to the other.

4-98. **com·pres′sion:** When you get a cut that bleeds, you need to put **compression** on it to get it to quit bleeding. You have *to press* on it until the bleeding stops.

4-99. **trans·mis′sion:** Dad said the **transmission** in his car needed more **transmission** fluid. He put in the fluid and the **transmission** started shifting correctly. The **transmission** *transfers* power from the engine to the wheels.

4-100. **de·pres′sion:** **Depression** is *a terrible feeling that things are bad and never going to get better.* Take time everyday to think of happy things, and you will see that **depression** will begin to disappear.

4-101. **ex·pres′sion:** A good rhetoric class can help you improve your **expression**. **Expression** is the *ability to express* yourself and let people know what you think and how you feel.

4-102. **im·pres′sion:** You can make a good **impression** on your teacher by doing good work at school. Your teacher will take note of your good work and reward you with good grades. She will have a good *opinion* of you.

4-103. **pro·gres′sion:** All good reading teachers know that there is a proper **progression** for teaching the sounds represented by the letters. They start with the simple and then move to the more complex.

4-104. **con·fes′sion:** They say that **confession** is good for you. If you do something you shouldn't, it will be easier in the long run to go ahead and *tell* your parents or teacher what you did wrong.

4-105. **ad·mis´sion:** To get into the theater, you need to purchase an **admission** ticket. You buy it at the **admission** window. You must have an admission ticket to *get in* to see the play.

4-106. **pre·ten´sion:** Jim gave his speech simply and without any **pretension**. He presented his ideas simply without *claiming to be anybody special*. He used simple, plain language. He did not use big complicated words to impress people. He let the facts speak for themselves.

4-107. **com·pul´sion:** Roger felt no **compulsion** to run any faster in the race. He did not feel *compelled* or motivated to run any faster. He was happy just to finish the long marathon.

4-108. **ap·pre·hen´sion:** An **apprehension** is *an anxiety or fear that something bad or unpleasant is going to happen*. Berry had an **apprehension** that the was going to get a C on the spelling test for which he failed to study.

4-109. **com·pre·hen´sion:** John's **comprehension** was poor. He *did not understand* the question the teacher was asking him. He couldn't **comprehend** because she used some words that he hadn't learned yet. To comprehend is *to understand*. Learn a lot of words and your comprehension will improve.

4-110. **ten´sion:** Jim felt a lot of **tension** in his shoulders from writing so long. His teacher told him to take a break and let his shoulders relax so the **tension** and *stress* would go away.

Chapter 5

Romance **Roots**

Romances (Latin/French) Elements of English
From the Golden Tongued Cicero
And the Mighty Roman Legions

Introduction to Latin Roots

A **root** is the main part of a word, the part to which the prefixes and suffixes are added. The root usually receives the accent in Latin based words.

Roots are valuable patterns for decoding and spelling.

Roots are also very valuable for learning new vocabulary to enhance your reading, writing, listening, and speaking ability.

Example: **reporter:** re·port·er

re is a <u>prefix</u> meaning *to repeat.*
port is a <u>root</u> meaning *to carry.*
er is a <u>suffix</u> indicating *agent.*

rupt
(to break, to burst)

5-1. **rup´ture:** The waterline to our house froze and had a **rupture**. It *broke* and the water came roaring out.

5-2. **e·rupt´:** During World War II, Mr. Potter's father saw Mount Vesuvius **erupt**. He saw smoke, fire, and lava *thrown out* of the mighty volcano.

5-3. **e·rup´tion:** Mr. Potter's dad, Orson Potter, saw a powerful **eruption** of the mighty volcano Vesuvius. He also saw the ancient buried Roman city of Pompeii.

5-4. **cor·rupt´:** The banker was **corrupt**. He had been stealing some of the money that people put in his bank. He was willing to *act dishonestly in return for money.*

5-5. **cor·rup´tion:** Some people say **corruption** is rampant in politics. They say that *dishonest* politicians buy citizens' votes with promises they never intend keep.

5-6. **bank´rupt:** A person who is **bankrupt** has no money in the bank to pay his bills. He has to tell people he can't pay them what he owes them. His *bank account is empty.*

5-7. **a·brupt´ly:** Mary **abruptly** broke off her engagement with Bill when she found out that he never worked a day in his life. *All of a sudden*, she quit seeing him.

5-8. **in·ter·rupt´:** You should never **interrupt** adults when they are talking. You should never *break* into their conversation with your comments or questions.

5-9. **dis·rupt´:** The rioters tried to **disrupt** the Governor when he was giving a speech. They tried to *interfere* with him speaking.

5-10. **dis·rup´tive:** Martha was very **disruptive** in history class. She **disrupted** the class by asking silly questions to make her friends laugh. The teacher was not able to teach the lesson. Martha said she was sorry.

5-11. **ir·rupt´:** The funny joke made the whole class **irrupt** in laughter. They suddenly *broke into* uncontrollable laughter.

5-12. **in·ter·rupt´ion:** Mrs. Pearl Monroe did not allow any **interruptions** during instruction. She would not let anyone *interfere with* her teaching. I should know. She was my first-grade teacher in Southern Indiana in 1953.

port
(to carry)

5-13. **im·port´:** **Import** means to *carry in*. Mom and Dad bought a car from Japan. They had to **import** it to the USA.

5-14. **ex·port´:** **Export** is the opposite of import. The United States **exports** a lot of cotton to other countries. They *send it out* to them.

5-15. **port´a·ble:** Something that is **portable** is something you are *able to carry*. A **portable** computer is small enough that you *can carry it* around from place to place.

5-16. **trans-port´**: Mary said she could **transport** the children to the ball game. She could *take them there* in her car.

5-17. **por´ter:** The **porter** carried our luggage to our hotel room. A **porter** is someone who *carries* things for you.

5-18. **de·port´:** The police sometimes have to **deport** people who are in our country illegally. They are *carried back* to their country.

5-19. **re·port´:** The reporter *gave an account of the events of the day.* He gave a **report** that was published in the morning paper.

5-20. **sup·port´:** Mr. Potter appreciates all the wonderful people who **support** him in his efforts to teach all boys and girls to read. To **support** is *to help.*

form
(to shape)

5-21. **re·form´:** Mr. Potter is trying to **reform** education so everyone can learn to read with phonics-first and not have to guess. He wants to *change it for the better.*

5-22. **in·form´:** We had to **inform** the teacher that there was a water pipe leaking in the bathroom. She was glad for the information. To **inform** is *to give facts or information.*

5-23. **de·form´:** Sarah once had a cat that was **deformed.** It was born with only three legs. Sarah loved it anyway and gave it a warm, loving home. It was *not formed right.*

5-24. trans´form: Mr. Potter thinks he can **transform** reading instruction by getting all the schools to use <u>Reading Made Easy with Blend Phonics</u> and <u>Beyond Blend Phonics</u>. He thinks he can *change* the way kids are taught to read so they can read better.

5-25. con´form: Mrs. Monroe explained that when we **conform** to her rules we will learn more. My Dad obeyed her rules, and he was really smart. So I plan to **conform** to her rules and see if I can get as smart as my Dad.

5-26. form´u·la: Charles Goodyear discovered a special **formula** or *recipe* for making rubber tires in 1844. Our cars and trucks have been rolling on rubber tires ever since.

5-27. in·for´mal: The teacher said we could wear blue jeans to school tomorrow. We do not have to dress **formal.** We can dress **informal. Informal** is also *casual.*

5-28. in·for´ma·tive: I read a very **informative** book about the history of aviation. The book was filled with **information** about all kinds of airplanes.

tract
(pull)

5-29. trac´tor: Mr. Potter's dad drove a Ford **tractor** on the farm. The **tractor** could *pull* a three bottom plow. Mr. Potter used to enjoy riding on the fender of the **tractor** while his father was plowing the fields.

5-30. trac´tion: When Jack broke his arm they had to put it in **traction.** They put it in a cast and tied a rope to it. The rope had a weight on the end that *pulls* on his arm to keep it straight. That's **traction!**

5-31. **at·tract´:** The gravity of the earth is able to **attract** the moon so that it does not go flying out of the solar system. The moon is *drawn to* the earth by gravity.

5-32. **at·trac´tive:** Mary is very **attractive.** She is very pretty and very nice to be around. People are naturally *drawn to* her. They like to be around her.

5-33. **ex·tract´:** The dentist had to **extract** John's tooth because it was hurting him. He *pulled* it out. Now he feels fine.

5-34. **con·trac´tual:** We signed the contact for the house. That made it a **contractual** agreement. The owner agreed to accept our money each month, and we agreed to pay.

5-35. **sub·tract´:** **Subtract** is another name for *take away.* We **subtract** when we take two from five and get three: 5 - 3 = 2.

5-36. **pro·tract´:** They decided to **protract** the School Board meeting. They decided to *meet longer* than they had planned.

5-37. **dis·tract´:** Do not **distract** your dad when he is driving in heavy traffic. Don't cause him to *loose his attention.*

5-38. **con·tract´:** My brother signed a **contract** to build a house for my uncle. He signed a paper to assure my uncle that he would build it for the price they had agreed upon.

scrib, scrip
(to write)

5-39. **scrib´ble:** When students first learn to write, their writing looks more like **scribble.** To **scribble** means to *write* or *draw carelessly* or *hurriedly.*

5-40. **a·scribe´:** Milton said he could **ascribe** his bad grade in spelling to a stomachache. He said his stomachache *caused him* to get a bad score. He *blamed* his bad score on the headache.

5-41. **de·scribe´:** Mary tried to **describe** her new puppy to the class. She told them what it *looked like.* It was a cute, black and white female Border Collie that loved to play.

5-42. **in·scribed´:** They **inscribed** the teacher's name on a plaque that they gave her for her retirement. They *wrote* her name on the plaque. She was a great teacher.

5-43. **pre·scribed´:** The doctor **prescribed** bed rest for Jackie, who had the flu at school last week. The doctor wrote a note to Jackie's mom that Jackie should rest in bed.

5-44. **cir·cum·scribe´:** The teacher strictly **circumscribed** the places on the playground where the kids could play. She told them where they could play and where they could not play. To **circumscribe** is *to restrict something within limits.*

5-45. **in·scrip´tion:** We read the **inscription** on the Civil War Monument when we were in Washington last summer. To *inscribe* means *to write* or *carve* words permanently on something. The **inscription** honored the brave men who fought for their country.

5-46. su·per·scrip´tion: A **superscription** is an inscription on the top of a document. The words "TOP SECRET" at the top of a secret diplomatic correspondence (letter) is a **superscription.**

5-47. script: **Script** is *handwriting* as distinct from print. It can also be a **script** for a play. Mary memorized her part in the **script** for the play they were to present at school.

5-48. Scrip´ture: Almost all world religions have **Scripture** that tell what they believe. The *sacred writings* of Christianity are contained in the Holy Bible.

5-49. tran·script´: A transcription is written or printed material that was first presented in another medium. Tim made a **transcript** of the teacher's notes from the chalkboard into his notebook. He copied the notes.

5-50. de·scrip´tive: Alice wrote a **descriptive** essay that told all about the beautiful hills of Kentucky. She *described* the bluegrass, tall trees, fast horse, and flowing rivers.

spec, spect
(to see, to watch)

5-51. spe´cies: There are many **species** of fish in the sea. There are many *kinds of* fish.

5-52. spe´cial: Mrs. Thelma Collins had a **special** treat for us today. She made pumpkin pie with whipped cream. She said it was a **special** treat for her **special** students.

5-53. **spe´ci·men:** Mrs. Collins brought several **specimens** of butterflies for us to look at under the magnifying glass. She brought *samples* for us to see.

5-54. **spec·ta´tor:** John was a **spectator** at the football game. He sat in the stands and *watched* the football game.

5-55. **spec·ta´cu·lar:** John said the football game was **spectacular.** It was lots of fun to watch because of the great playing. It was *very impressive.*

5-56. **re·spect´:** Mr. Potter had a great deal of **respect** for Mrs. Pearl Monroe because she taught him to read well with phonics in first-grade. He *regarded her highly.*

5-57. **re·spect´ful:** Mary was **respectful** of her college professors. She had a lot of respect for them because they taught her what she needed to learn. She was *full of respect.*

5-58. **dis·re·spect´ful:** We should never be **disrespectful** to our elders. They deserve our respect and appreciation because they have worked hard to helped us to be better people. Disrespect is a *lack of respect or courtesy.*

stru, strut
(to build)

5-59. **in´stru·ment:** Mr. Potter plays two **instruments.** He plays the harmonica and the guitar. Mr. Potter recommends that everyone play a music **instrument.** He says it makes you smarter and happier.

5-60. **struc´ture:** The Capitol building is an imposing **structure.** It is a very impressive *building.* You can't miss it.

5-61. **struc′tu·ral:** The **structural** integrity of the building is sound. It was built to withstand an earthquake. It will not fall in an earthquake because it is very strong.

5-62. **con·struct′:** My dad decided to **construct** his own house. He *built* it himself.

5-63. **con-struc′tion:** Dad told us to be careful around the **construction** site. He said the power tools they use to construct the building could be dangerous. To construct is to build. A **construction** is *something that has been built.*

5-64. **re·con·struc′tion·ist: reconstructionist,** what a big word. Let's look at every part: re-con-**struc**-tion-ist. That's easier! It is a person who helps with the *rebuilding of a structure or building.*

5-65. **in·struct′:** Our teacher is trying to **instruct** us in the fine art of sewing. She is *teaching* us how to sew.

5-66. **in·struc′tor:** Mr. Potter is our Spanish **instructor.** He is our Spanish *teacher.* He instructs us in Spanish.

5-67. **in·struc′tive:** Yesterday we learned a very **instructive** handwriting lesson. Mr. Potter *showed us how to use* a dip pen to write beautiful cursive letters.

5-68. **ob·struct′:** The rioters tried to **obstruct** the traffic by putting a tree across the road. They were trying to *block* the traffic so no one could get by. The police removed the tree.

5-69. **de·struc′tive:** A **destructive** wind blew down the power lines. We did not have electricity for three days. The wind *destroyed* a lot of electric power lines.

dic, dict
(to say, to tell)

5-70. **in·di·cate′:** The coach wanted to **indicate** to the quarterback that it was time for the new play. He held up two fingers *to show* the quarterback what he wanted him to do.

5-71. **in·di·ca′tion:** The quarterback gave no **indication** that he knew what the coach wanted, so the coach called timeout. He told the quarterback what he had been trying to *indicate* to him. An **indication** is a *sign*.

5-72. **in·di·ca′tor:** The wind direction **indicator** indicated that the wind was coming out of the north. It *showed* the direction from which the wind was coming.

5-73. **dic′tate:** A dictator likes to **dictate** what all the people have to do. He likes to *tell them what to do*, and they have to do it. Dictators can be very nasty people, trying to control everything people do.

5-74. **dic·ta′tor:** *A person who dictates* is called a **dictator.** There were several really bad **dictators** in the twentieth-century *who told their citizens what to do all the time.*

5-75. **pre·dict′:** The weatherman tries to **predict** what the weather is going to do. He tries to tell us if it is going to be rainy or sunny. To **predict** is *to tell beforehand.*

5-76. **pre·dic′tion:** The weatherman makes his **prediction** based on a lot of meteorological data. He looks at all the data to figure out what is *going to happen* tomorrow.

5-77. **dic′tion:** Mr. Monroe worked very hard to teach us good **diction** so people would not make fun of our speech. She taught us never to say, "I ain't got no money!"

5-78. **dic′tum:** A **dictum** *is a short saying that expresses a general truth or principal.* "Don't count your chickens until they hatch." is an example of a **dictum.**

5-79. **con·tra·dic′tion:** There was a **contradiction** in Jimmy's story about how he lost his homework. He claimed his dog ate it, but he didn't even own a dog!

5-80. **in·dict′:** The judge decided to **indict** the man for entering into a house and stealing jewelry. He was *formally charged* with the crime. He went to trial and then to jail.

flext, flex
(to bend)

5-81. **in·flect′:** <u>Beyond Blend Phonics</u> is teaching you how to **inflect** words to change their meaning with roots, prefixes, and suffixes.

5-82. **re·flect′:** A mirror can **reflect** the light of the sun. Boy Scouts use mirrors to **reflect** light to send signals to each other in Morse code. The mirror *throws back* the light.

5-83. **in·flec′tion:** Our speech teacher showed us how the **inflection** of our voice could help us communicate emotion and sincerity. To inflect the voice is to *change the pitch.*

5-84 **de·flect′:** The warrior's metal shield was able to **deflect** the arrow. It sent the arrow going in the opposite direction. It *bounced right off* the strong shield.

5-85. **re·flec´tor:** I have a **reflector** on the back of my bicycle so people can see me after dark. The **reflector** can *reflect* light. This makes my bike easier to see in the dark.

5-86. **flex:** Boys like to **flex** their muscles to show how strong they are. They make a muscle with their arms. **Flex** means to *bend*.

5-87. **flex´i·ble:** Everyone should do stretching exercises everyday to keep their body **flexible**. A **flexible** body can *bend* without getting hurt.

5-88. **re´flex:** Reading should become a **reflex**. A **reflex** is *something we can do automatically:* fast & accurately. You have to read some everyday to develop a good reading **reflex**.

5-89. **cir´cum-flex:** Mr. Potter also teaches Ancient Greek. The Greeks write a **circumflex** accent over some of their vowels. ὑμεῖς is the Greek word for "you." The ˆ over the Greek letter ι is a **circumflex** accent.

mit, miss
(to send)

5-90. **ad·mit´:** They would not **admit** my brother into the hospital because he forgot his insurance card. A friend ran home to get the card so the hospital could **admit** my brother. **Admit** means to *let in*. It can also mean *to confess something is true.*

5-91. **com·mit´:** Steve would not **commit** to the discipline necessary to learn to read Ancient Hebrew so he learned Ancient Greek instead. To **commit** is to *pledge* or *agree to do something.*

5-92. **o·mit´:** Don't **omit** any important details from your report on the Mayflower crossing the Atlantic. Don't *leave out* anything important.

5-93. **re·mit´:** They failed to add the postage so the company wouldn't send the package until they **remitted** the postage. They would not *send* them the package till they received the postage.

5-94. **per´mit:** You have to get a **permit** from the Principal to park on the school parking lot. You have to get *signed permission* to park there. Here **permit** is a <u>noun</u>.

5-95. **per·mit´:** "Will your father **permit** you to go to the library with me tomorrow?" asked Tom. "Sure," I said. He will *allow* me to *go* to the library to read a good book. Here **permit** is a <u>verb</u>.

5-96. **sub·mit´:** You can **submit** your poem to the newspaper to see if they will publish it. You can *give it to them to consider* for publication.

5-97. **trans·mit´:** The Amateur Radio Operator was able to **transmit** an important message in Morse Code. He *sent* the Morse Code message by shortwave radio.

5-98. **mis´sion:** The brave astronauts went on a **mission** to the moon. They were *sent* there to learn what they could about the moon's history and composition.

5-99. **mis´sive:** Field Marshal Montgomery sent a **missive** to his Captains to hold off the attack for two more hours. He sent them a *formal letter* to stop the attack for two hours.

5-100. **ad·mis´sion:** The **admission** to the movie was only $3.00. It *cost* three-dollars *to get in* to see the movie.

5-101. **dis·miss´:** Our Principal had to **dismiss** the kids from school early today so they could get home before the bad storm struck. She *allowed them to leave* early.

5-102. **re·miss´:** I would be **remiss** if I didn't do everything I can to help all my students learn to read well. I would be *neglecting my duty* if I didn't help them.

cred
(to believe)

5-103. **cred´it:** You have to have good **credit** before the bank will loan you money. They have to *believe* you can pay the money back before they will loan you the money.

5-104. **dis·cred´it:** We had to **discredit** Jim when he told us that he had ridden on the back of a fire breathing dragon. We did *not believe* his incredible story.

5-105. **ac·cred´it:** The teacher was able to **accredit** Mary with being the best speller in the school. She *gave* her *credit* for being the best speller when she won the Spelling Bee.

5-106. **cred´i·tor:** John is the **creditor** to almost everyone in the classroom. He is always loaning the money to other kids. A **creditor** is *one who loans money.*

5-107. **cre·den´tial:** Dad had to show the airline that he had his **credentials**. He had to *prove that he was who he said he was.* He showed them his Passport and Drivers' License.

5-108. cred´i·ble: John is **credible.** He always tells the truth. Everyone *believed* him when he said that he was eight years old. He is an honest boy.

5-109. in·cred´i·ble: John told us an **incredible** story about how he found a baby dragon under his bed and kept his find secret from everyone. We *didn't believe* his story.

5-110. ac·cred·i·ta´tion: The new school has full **accreditation.** All the teachers have their certifications and the students' credits transfer to all the other schools in the state.

pend
(hang)

5-111. pen´ding: The students' passing to the next grade is **pending** until their grades are all in. They are *waiting for* report cards to se if they are going to pass.

5-112. pen´du·lum: The **pendulum** on the grandfather clock was swinging back and forth, singing, "Tick-Tock" over and over all day long. The pendulum is a *hanging weight* that swings left and right.

5-113. de·pen´da·bil·i·ty: Everyone should develop **dependability** in their life. They should learn to be responsible so others can *depend* and *rely* on them to do what they say they are going to do. Are you *dependable*?

5-114. pen´dant: Mary wore a **pendant** to school. She wore a necklace with a little owl *hanging down* on a gold chain. It was so cute!

5-115. de·pen′dent: We are **dependent** on our first-grade teacher to teach us how to read with phonics. We *depend* on her. If she doesn't teach us phonics, we might never learn.

5-116. in·de·pen′dent: Mary is very **independent**. She does not need much help with spelling because she can learn the word all by herself. She *doesn't depend* on anyone.

5-117. sus-pend′: The custodian was able to **suspend** the new light from the ceiling. He *hung* the light from the ceiling.

duc, duce, duct
(to lead)

5-118. e·du′cate: To **educate** a child is to *lead* them to learn. A good teacher is a good educational *leader.*

5-119. de·duce′: The teacher **deduced** that Mark stole Mike's ruler because it was in his desk and had his fingerprints on it. She *concluded from the evidence* that Mark took it. She made him give it back.

5-120. re·duce′: Harriet said she was going to **reduce**. She was going to *loose* weight by doing more walking. That's a good way to **reduce** weight.

5-121. in·tro·duce′: Let me **introduce** you to my best friend. His name is Pete. He helped me a lot when I taught Spanish speaking boys and girls how to speak and read English. To **introduce** is *to make someone known by name.*

5-122. in-duce′: Jerry's mother **induced** him to do all his homework by promising to take him to a movie every month. She *influenced* him to do his work by promising the reward

5-123. **pro·duce´:** The science class was able to **produce** a car that ran on gas made from corn. They *made* a model car that ran on corn gas. Maybe you will drive a car that runs on gas made from corn someday. To **produce** is *to make.*

5-124. **con´duct:** Mark's **conduct** grade went up the last six weeks. He has been *behaving* better in class. Your **conduct** is *your behavior.*

5-125. **de·duct´:** Mrs. Stowe had to **deduct** five points from Judy's grade for not signing the paper. She *took off* five points from her grade because Judy forgot to sign the paper.

5-126. **re·duc´tion:** A five point **reduction** of a grade for forgetting to sign my name would really hurt. I never forget to sign my name because I do not want my grade *lowered!*

pel
(to drive, to push)

5-127. **im·pel´:** The propeller on John's toy airplane was able to **impel** if forward fast enough to win the model airplane race. It *drove* the plane forward really fast.

5-128. **com·pel´:** We could not **compel** dad to let us to the movies with our friends. We could not *convince* Dad to let us go. He took us fishing instead, which was more fun!

5-129. **ex·pel´:** The teacher had to **expel** Raymond when he refused to obey her. She *made him leave* the class. His dad made Raymond apologize and promise to obey his teacher. He learned a good lesson and was never **expelled** again.

5-130. **pro·pel′:** The mighty Saturn V Rocket Engine was able to **propel** the Apollo Spacecraft to the moon. It was able to *push* the heavy craft into lunar orbit.

5-131. **dis·pel′:** Mrs. Conrad was able to **dispel** the students' fear of garden snakes. She showed them that the garden snakes were harmless and actually made nice pets. She made their fear *go away.*

5-132. **re·pel′:** Dad put mosquito repellant on us, when we went outside, to help **repel** the mosquitoes. To **repel** means to *drive* or *force away.* We didn't want to get bitten.

puls
(to drive, to push)

5-133. **im·pulse′:** John had an irresistible **impulse** to laugh in class when Mark spilled his ink on the floor. He had a *strong desire* to laugh, but he controlled himself and just smiled. John even helped Mark cleanup the mess.

5-134. **com·pul′sion:** Mr. Potter once had a **compulsion** to play his harmonica in his fifth-grade classroom. He had a strong *urge* or *desire* to play it. Bad idea!!!

5-135. **ex·pul′sion: Expulsion** from school is a severe form of discipline. **Expulsion** means the student was *kicked out* of his school. He was told to *leave* for some reason.

5-136. **pro·pul′sion:** A jet airplane has a jet engine for **propulsion. Propulsion** is the *act of driving* or *pushing forward.* Jet airplanes have powerful engines that propel planes through the air.

5-137. **im·pul´sive:** Martha is very **impulsive.** She often talks without thinking. She says and does things *without thinking* about the consequences. Slowdown Martha!

fac, fact
(to make, to do)

5-138. **fac´ul·ty:** Mr. Potter's elementary school had a **faculty** of four teachers for eight grades. Each teacher taught two grades. **Faculty** means *teaching staff.*

5-139. **fac´ile:** **Facile** is usually pronounced /fă-sŭl/. Mr. Potter usually uses **facile** in the sense of something that is *easy.* It can also mean *superficial* or *shallow.*

5-140. **fa·ci´li·ty:** John had a tremendous **facility** for languages. He had the ability to learn them *easily.*

5-141. **fa·ci·li·tate´:** John purchased a computer to **facilitate** the writing of his research paper. The computer would *make it easier* for him to write the paper.

5-142. **fact:** Is it a **fact** that Spanish is easier to read and spell than English? Yes, Tommy, it is *true* that Spanish is easier to read and spell than English.

5-143. **man·u·fac´ture:** Mrs. Henry told us that they **manufacture** chairs in the factory downtown. They *make* beautiful chairs there.

5-144. **fac´to·ry:** They manufacture chairs in the **factory.** A **factory** is a building or group of buildings where things are assembled (put together, *made*), chiefly by machine.

5-145. sat·is·fac′tion: Mr. Potter gets an immense amount of **satisfaction** teaching boys and girls to how to read without guessing. It makes him *feel good* to see them enjoying learning to reading better.

vert, vers
(to turn)

5-146. con·vert′: The chair factory can **convert** raw materials like wood and metal into very conformable and nice looking chairs. They can *change* the raw materials into chairs. (A **con′vert** is *a person who has been converted.*)

5-147. con-ver′ti·ble: My uncle drives a **convertible**. He can drive his car with the top up or down. When the top is down, you can feel the breeze. He can convert it from a car with a top to a car without a top. To convert means *to change.*

5-148. in′tro·vert: Introvert is a word often used to describe a *shy person.* A *shy* person is uncomfortable around a lot of people. They prefer a few close friends rather than a crowd. They tend to *look inside* instead of outside.

5-149. di·vert′: The airport had to **divert** the airplane from its path because there was a dangerous storm in the way. They *changed direction* to be safe.

5-150. ex′tro·vert: An **extrovert** is the opposite of an introvert. The **extrovert** likes to be around lots of people and always has lots of friends. Extroverts are *not shy.*

5-151. **con·ver′sion:** In schools these days, they teach students the **conversion** of metric units to US Customary units. They learn to convert or *change* from one to another.

5-152. **di·ver′sion:** Mr. Potter types a lot and gets pretty tired sometimes so he stops and takes a little **diversion** by playing his guitar. A **diversion** is *something fun* you do that is good for your mind and body.

5-153. **a·ver′sion:** Mr. Potter has an **aversion** to skunks because of their bad odor. He has a *strong dislike* for them and avoids them because they stink.

ject
(to throw)

5-154. **ob′ject:** My dog dragged a large **object** into the yard. It was the neighbor's big flower pot. The flowers were all over the yard. I told the my neighbor that I was sorry. An **object** is a *thing*. (To **ob·ject′** is *to disagree*.)

5-155. **pro·ject′:** Our teacher bought a new projector so she could **project** a picture or text on the overhead screen in our room. By *throwing* the picture on the screen, she was able to hold our interest and teach us more. (A **pro′ject** is a *plan* for accomplishing something.)

5-156. **de·jec′ted:** Sam felt **dejected** because no one would play with him at recess. He was *sad* and *lonely* because he had to play all by himself at recess.

5-157. **re·jec′ted:** My research paper was **rejected** because I forgot to follow the correct format. The teacher sent my research paper back to me because I forgot to used the correct format. I made the correction and got a good grade.

5-158. **ob·jec´tive:** The **objective** of the math assignment was to help us master double digit multiplication. The *goal* was to teach us to solve harder multiplication problems.

5-159. **e·jec´tion:** The **ejection** seat worked perfectly in the test plane. The pilots can trust the **ejection** mechanism to work fine in an emergency. It will *throw* the pilots out of the airplane so they can parachute to the ground safely.

5-160. **pro·jec´tion:** The new projector made a big **projection** on the huge screen at the front of the room. It *throws* the pictures and text on the big screen so everyone can see it.

5-161. **pro·jec´tor:** Our teacher thanked Mr. Elliott for buying a **projector** for our classroom. He is a great guy, and the **projector** is a wonderful addition to our classroom. It *throws* a great image on the screen.

5-162. **re·jec´tion:** **Rejection** is the noun form of the verb reject. Mary experienced **rejection** when the boys and girls did not want to play with her. They *rejected* her.

5-163. **ob·jec´tion:** The teacher asked the students if anyone had an **objection** to having a picnic next Friday. She wanted to know if anyone had a *reason against* a picnic.

5-164. **in·jec´tion:** An **injection** is a *shot*. Mark had to have weekly **injections** to help him get over his allergies.

5-165. **pro·jec´tile:** At the Track Meet the javelin thrower threw his **projectile** farther than anyone else. A **projectile** is anything *thrown* through the air, especially a weapon.

5-166. **in·ter-ject´:** Jim felt bound to **interject** his opinion in the discussion. He felt he had to *insert* or *give* his opinion right then and there.

5-167. **in·ter·jec´tion:** An **interjection** is one of the eight parts of speech we learn in English class. It is an *abrupt remark*. We also call it an *exclamation*. This is the last Latin root we will study! You can now read many English words with Latin roots.

Chapter 6

Greek **Combining Forms**

From the days of the Greek Philosophers
Socrates, Plato, and Aristotle.

phon, phono
(sound, voice)

6-1. **te·le·phone´:** Alexander Graham Bell invented the
telephone. The telephone carries our voice long
distances over wire by electrical means. **Tele** means *long*.

6-2. **pho´neme:** Linguistics call the irreducible sounds of
spoken language **phonemes**. There are three phonemes
in the word *back*: /b/ /ă/ /k/. It is spelled "back."

6-3. **phon´ics: Phonics** is *a method of teaching people to read
by correlating sounds with letters or groups of letters in an
alphabetic writing system.* **Phonics** is a plural noun treated
as singular. **Phonics** is the only right way to teach
beginning reading.

6-4. **pho·ne´tics: Phonetics** is *the study and classification of
speech sounds.* A good phonics teacher will know his or her
phonetics. **Phonetics** is a plural noun treated as
singular.

6-5. **pho´no·graph:** A **phonograph** is a machine for
playing vinyl records. The word literally means *write with
sounds.* A needle sense the sounds inscribed in the
grooves.

6-6. **pho´no·gram:** A **phonogram** is a *symbol representing
a spoken sound.* Words ending like *ate, ite, ote, ete, ute* in the
words **late, mite, Pete,** and **lute** are called **phonograms**.

6-7. **pho´no·l·gy:** Can you figure out the meaning of
this word? Hint: The suffix -ology means study.
Phonology is the *study of speech sounds.*

photo
(light)

6-8. **pho′to·co·py:** A **photocopy** is made on a photocopier that uses the action of light on a specially prepared surface *to copy the printed material.*

6-9. **pho·tog′ra·phy:** My sister took a **photography** class in college. She learned to take really good pictures with a camera. She also learned to process the pictures in a darkroom. It literally means *to write with light.*

6-10. **pho·to·flash′:** A **photoflash** will enable you to take a picture in the dark. The flashbulb lights up and makes enough light for you to take a picture in the dark.

6-11. **pho·to′-gra·pher:** My sister is a great **photographer.** She took a photography course at the local college and learned how to take great photographs. A photographer is a person who takes pictures.

auto
(self)

6-12. **au·to·ma′tion:** The car company has introduced a lot of **automation** to its car assembly line. The machines put the car together automatically without anybody touching the parts. **Automation** is *the use of automatic machines to make things.*

6-13. **au·to·ma′tic:** Dad bought Mom an **automatic** dishwasher so she doesn't have to wash the dishes anymore by hand. She just puts the dishes in the dishwasher, and the dishwater washes the dishes all *by itself.*

6-14. **au´to·graph:** Everyone's **autograph** is different. No two people sign their name exactly the same. A handwriting expert can always identify your **autograph.** *John Hancock* is the most famous autograph in American history.

6-15. **au´to·mo·bile´:** An **automobile** can take you almost anywhere you want to go. An **automobile** is a vehicle with a motor that can *move itself.* It is also called a *car.*

tele
(distance)

6-16. **te·le·cast´:** They had an all-night **telecast** last night on TV to raise money to help children with physical problems. They had a television broadcast to raise the money.

6-17. **te·le·phone´:** A **telephone** lets us talk to our friends who are a *long way off.* Today most people use cell phones that use radio waves instead of wires to carry voice over long distances.

6-18. **te·le·gram´:** A **telegram** is *a message delivered in written or printed form.* One day they brought my Mom a **telegram** that let us know that Uncle John was coming to visit us.

6-19. **te·le·pho´to:** Marge's new camera has a **telephoto** lens that enables her to take pictures of things that are *far away.* The **telephoto** lens makes *distant* things look closer.

6-20. **te´le·graph:** Samuel Morse invented the **telegraph** years ago. He created a special code of dots (.) and dashes (_): SOS = (..._ _ _...). Mr. Potter is a high speed code operator. His Amateur Radio call sign is NG5W.

6-21. **te´le·thon:** Gerry Lewis used to have a **telethon** to help children. A **telethon** is *a very long television program, usually one broadcast for raising money to help other people.*

graph, gram
(letter, writing)

6-22. **pho´no·graph:** Mr. Potter's parents bought him a little **phonograph** that played phonograph records. Records were vinyl disks that had grooves on them that contained the sound of the songs. A needle rested in the groove as the record rotated round and round.

6-23. **pho´to·graph:** A **photograph** is a kind of drawing on paper with light. light + drawing = **photo-graph.**

6-24. **pho·tog´ra·pher:** A **photographer** is a person who takes photographs. My wife loves *to take* a lot of *photographs* of our family. She is a **photographer.**

6-25. **te·le´gra·phy:** The telegraph is a machine for sending a message with Morse Code. There are a lot of Amateur Radio operators that send **telegraphy** messages with Morse Code.

6-26. **gra´phics:** Modern computer games have great **graphics.** Mr. Potter has a Flight Simulator that is almost as realistic as flying a real airplane.

ology
(study)

6-27. **pho´no·lo·gy:** If you want to know the sounds of a language, you *study* the science of **phonology. Phonology** is *the study the speech sounds of a language.*

6-28. **psy·cho·lo·gy:** The **psychology** of reading is the *study* of how the mind functions in reading. Mr. Potter studies the **psychology** of reading so he can be a better reading teacher. **Psychology** is *the scientific study of the human mind.*

6-29. **bi·ol´o·gy: Biology** is the *study of living things.* In school, we *study* plants and animals in our **biology** class.

6-30. **zo·ol´o·gy: Zoology** is *the scientific study of animals.* A **zoologist** is a person who studies animals. You can see lots of different kinds of animals in a zoo.

6-31. **ge·ol´o·gy: Geology** is *the study of the earth.* There are a lot of different kinds of rocks and minerals. Geologists study them all. Some rocks are soft, some are hard, some are very beautiful.

audio
(sound)

6-32. **au·di·om´e·ter:** Many factories these days install **audiometers** *to measure the sound level* in their factories. Too much noise can ruin your ability to hear so it is important to keep the noise down to a safe level.

6-33. **au·di·o·vis´u al:** An educational movie is an **audiovisual** method for teaching a lesson. We use both our senses of *hearing and seeing* at the same time to teach a subject with a movie. Kids usually like **audiovisual** methods.

micro
(small, little)

6-34. **mi´cro·scope´:** A biologist uses a **microscope** to see little animals that swim around in the water. A **microscope** <u>makes little things look big</u> so we can see them better. **Micro** means *little* and **scope** means *watch*.

6-35. **mi·crom´e·ter:** A **micrometer** allows an engineer or mechanic *to measure very small things.* If you ever work on a car motor, you will be using a **micrometer.**

meter
(measure)

6-36. **ba·rom´e·ter:** The weather man uses a **barometer** *to measure air pressure.* Knowing changes in air pressure can help the weatherman predict the weather.

6-37. **spee·dom´e·ter:** Every car has a **speedometer** so that the driver can know how fast he or she is going. A **speedometer** *measures how fast* the car is going.

6-38. **pe·dom´e·ter:** I have a **pedometer** it helps *measures the distance that I walk or run by counting the number of steps. Ped* is from the Greek word for *"foot."*

6-39. **ther·mom´e·ter:** The nurse has a **thermometer** in her office. She uses it to *measure body temperature* to see if we are sick. A high temperature is a sign of a fever.

therm
(heat)

6-40. **ther′mal:** Mom bought me some **thermal** socks and gloves. They provide great insulation against the cold. They keep my hands and feet *warm* in the coldest weather.

6-41. **ther′mo·dy·nam′ics:** Today we were studying how the internal combustion engine in the car works. Our teacher taught us the laws of **thermodynamics,** which explains the relationship between *heat* and other forms of energy.

bio
(life)

6-42. **au·to-bi·o-graph′i·cal:** Sir Winston Churchill wrote an **autobiographical** account of his life. The told *the story of his own life in his own words*. He was a outstanding leader in England during the Second World War.

6-43. **bi·o′gra·phy:** A **biography** is the *account of someone's life written by someone else*. Mr. Potter read Lord Charnwood's biography of Abraham Lincoln when Mr. Potter was in high school.

6-44. **au·to·bi·og′ra·phy:** A **biography** is *the account of a person's life written by that person*. Benjamin Franklin wrote one of the most famous **autobiographies** of all times. You should read it sometime.

6-45. **bi·ol′o·gy:** Biology is *the study of life*. Biologists study plants and animals to learn more about life on our planet.

scope
(watch)

6-46. **mi´cro·scope:** Jim got a **microscope** for his birthday. He could view tiny objects under the microscope. **Micro** mean *little* and **scope** means *watch* or *see*.

6-47. **te´le·scope:** With a good **telescope,** you can see the rings of Saturn. A **telescope** makes is possible for us to see things *far away* that we can't see with the eyes alone.

hydro
(water)

6-48. **hy´dro·gen: Hydrogen** is a gas that is lighter than air. It is highly explosive. They used to put it in big balloons called Dirigibles until one caught on fire in a bad storm.

6-49. **hy·drol´o·gy: Hydrology** is *the study of the movement of water.* We need to know how the movement of water in rivers is going to affect the life of people along the rivers. The water from a big flood can do a lot of damage.

6-50. **hy´dro·plane:** A **hydroplane** is a *light fast motorboat designed to skim over the surface of the water.* J. W. Whitlock's 1924 hydroplane, *Hoosier Boy,* set a speed record that still stands. He was an inventor from Rising Sun, Indiana.

6-51. **hy´dro·stat:** A **hydrostat** *controls water pressure* just like a **thermostat** controls the heat. I have a **hydrostat** on my water well to make sure the water pressure stays the same all the time.

6-52. **hy´drant:** Firemen can connect a fire hose to a fire **hydrant** to get water to put out a fire.

Chapter 7

Select Homonyms

Words that Sound Alike
but are Spelled Differently

Mostly Anglo-Saxon

roll – role

7-1. **roll**: 1. I had a delicious **roll** for dinner. Rolls are made of bread. 2. Jack can **roll** on the floor.

7-2. **role**: I was chosen to play the **role** of a prince in the school play. I will be playing the *part* of the Prince of Denmark. A **role** is a *part* in a play.

its – it's

7-3. **its**: The cat had **its** fur up because it was afraid of the mean dog.

7-4. **it's**: **It's** a good day today. *It is* a good day today. **It's** is a contraction for *it is*.

sun – son

7-5. **sun**: The **sun** in the sky is bright yellow and very hot.

7-6. **son**: Mr. Potter has a **son**. He likes to ride off-road motorcycles.

buy – by – bye

7-7. **buy:** Dad went with me to help me **buy** my first car.

7-8. **by:** Mr. Potter did not go **by** himself to buy his first car.

7-9. **bye:** Nathaniel told his mom, "**Bye**, see you tomorrow." **Bye** is short for goodbye.

cell – sell

7-10. **cell: 1.** The prisoner had to stay in his little jail **cell** until he had served his sentence. 2. Don't drive while texting on your **cell** phone

7-11. **sell:** Mark wanted to **sell** a lot of magazines so he could win the prize.

for – four

7-12. **for:** I washed dishes **for** my mom. **For** is a preposition.

7-13. **four:** There are **four** girls in my first-grade class. **Four** is a number adjective.

hour – our

7-14. **hour:** What **hour** is it? What *time* is it? It is five o'clock. **Hour** is a noun.

7-15. **our:** I do not know the hour because **our** clock is broken. **Our** is a possessive pronoun.

hole – whole

7-16. **hole:** My dog dug a big **hole** in the backyard.

7-17. **whole:** Mom bought a big watermelon, and we ate the **whole** thing in just one day. We ate it *all*.

led - lead

7-18. **led:** Dad **led** me to the old pond where he used to swim with his brother. He took my hand and *guided* me.

7-19. **lĕad:** The **lead** in the pencil lets us write on paper.

hear – here

7-20. **hear:** Did you **hear** what I said?

7-21. **here:** My bicycle is **here** on the back porch.

reed – read

7-22. **reed:** A clarinet uses a **reed** in the mouthpiece to create musical sound. The **reed** is a flat piece of wood that vibrates when you blow over it. **Reed** is, also, the name for a plant that grows in the water and has a flat leaf.

7-23. **rēad:** Phonics is the very best way to teach children to **read** well. Mr. Potter's students learn to **read** well.

sea – see

7-24. **sea:** Big ships cross the **sea** everyday.

7-25. **see:** You have to open your eyes if you want to **see**.

weather – whether

7-26. **weather:** The **weather** is very cold outside.

7-27. **whether:** Everyone wants to know **whether** you are going to the zoo with us or not.

hi – high

7-28. **hi:** Hi, James. How are you? **Hi** is another word for *hello*.

7-29. **high:** Dad asked me to climb **high** up in the tree to get down the kite my brother got caught in the limbs.

weak – week

7-30. **weak:** Jim was too **weak** to lift up the package. He had to get his big brother's help.

7-31. **week:** There are seven days in a **week**.

brake – break

7-32. **brake:** Dad checked the **brakes** on his truck to make sure they would stop his truck fast.

7-33. **break:** If you push too hard on your pencil point you will **break** the lead.

peace – piece

7-34. **peace:** Jim always tries to make **peace**. He helps everyone get along with each other.

7-35. **piece:** Mom gave me a big **piece** of delicious pumpkin pie.

cereal - serial

7-36. **cereal:** Judy likes a heaping bowl of delicious **cereal** for breakfast.

7-37. **serial:** J. R. Tolkien wrote a **serial** publication of three exciting books called *The Lord of the Rings*.

sail – sale

7-38. **sail:** I am going to **sail** my toy boat on the lake today. The boat had a big **sail**.

7-39. **sale:** Mom went to a **sale** today to see if she could save some money.

fair – fare

7-40. **fair:** I plan to go to the **fair** today to ride the rollercoaster.

7-41. **fare:** I had exactly three dollars for the bus **fare** to take me to the library.

too – two – to

7-42. **too:** I want to play outside, **too**. **Too** means *also*.

7-43. **two:** I have **two** dollars. **Two** is the number 2.

7-44. **to:** I was going **to** the store with Mom. She wanted me **to** go too. **To** is a preposition and the sign of an infinitive.

plain - plane

7-45. **plain:** Mr. Potter likes his yogurt **plain** without vanilla or anything mixed in.

7-46. **plane:** The jet fighter is a fast **plane**. **Plane** is short for airplane.

sew – so

7-47. **sew:** My grandmother wants to **sew** a beautiful dress for Mary. She has a new sewing machine.

7-48. **so:** I got really tired walking home **so** I stopped and took a little rest.

vain, vein, vane

7-49. **vain:** All our work was in **vain** because the motor didn't work.

7-50. **vein:** They give him a flu shot in the **vein** in his arm. Blood flows through the **veins**.

7-51. **vane:** The weather **vane** pointed north in the wind.

wood – would

7-52. **wood:** We burned **wood** in the fireplace to keep us warm. **Wood** comes from trees.

7-53. **would:** **Would** you be able to come to my house tomorrow to play rhythm guitar for the group?

rain – reign

7-54 **rain:** The weatherman said it would **rain** tomorrow.

7-55. **reign:** The **reign** of King Arthur was full of adventure.

knew – new

7-56. **knew:** I **knew** I was going to get an A on the test. I studied real hard.

7-57. **new:** Dad said he had a **new** book on rocket ships that he bought for me. It was recently published.

knows – nose

7-58. **knows:** No one **knows** what is going to happen tomorrow.

7-59. **nose:** Janet had a runny **nose** from an allergy that was bothering her.

know – no

7-60. **know:** Do you **know** anyone who can help me with my math?

7-61. **no:** **No**, I do not know anyone who can help you with your math, except me! I'll be glad to help.

write – right

7-62. **write:** Did you **write** your mom a letter to thank her for the gift?

7-63. **right:** Are you sure that you're **right** about the answer to that algebra problem?

hall –haul

7-64. **hall:** My locker is at the end of the **hall**.

7-65. **haul:** They put the new chairs on the truck to **haul** them to the school.

road – rode

7-66. **road:** The **road** repair crew is repairing holes in the **road**.

7-67. **rode:** Alexis **rode** her Quarter Horse in the parade last Friday.

board – bored

7-68. **board:** The carpenter sawed the wooden **board** to make the shelf.

7-69. **bored:** No one ever gets **bored** in Mr. Potter's reading class. Mr. Potter reads exciting books like *Bears of Blue River*.

loan – lone

7-70. **loan:** Can you **loan** me a dollar till I get my allowance next week?

7-71. **lone:** I saw a **lone** student walking across the parking lot. No one was with him. He was walking by himself.

way – weigh

7-72. **way:** My Aunt Marge Potter showed me the **way** to the Carnegie Library.

7-73. **weigh:** My veterinarian asked me to **weigh** my dog to see how much she weighs.

eight – ate

7-74. **eight:** I ate **eight** pretzels while watching the movie.

7-75. **ate:** Who **ate** the piece of pie that I left on the table?

their – there- they're

7-76. **their:** Students should do **their** own work. **Their** is possessive.

7-77. **there:** John says that **there** is a book on the table over **there**. **There** is an adverb: *in, at,* or *to* that place or position.

7-78. **they're: They're** is a contracted or shortened form of *they are.* **They're** going to town today.

your – you're

7-79. **your: Your** house is just down the street from mine. **Your** is possessive.

7-80. **you're:** I think **you're** learning to read really well. **You're** is a contracted form of *you are.*

steal – steel

7-81. **steal:** Mom taught my brother and me never to **steal**.

7-82. **steel:** The bucket was made out of **steel**, which is a really strong metal.

steak - stake

7-83. **steak:** We ate a really good **steak** at the restaurant.

7-84. **stake:** We use **stakes** tied to ropes to keep our tent from falling.

ant – aunt

7-85. **ant:** An **ant** is a little animal that lives in a nest under the ground.

7-86. **aunt:** My **Aunt** Mable Elliott buys me lots of books.

blue – blew

7-87. **blue:** My brother Ron's favorite color was **blue**.

7-88. **blew:** My brother Ron **blew** a trumpet in the band

capitol – capital

7-89. **capitol:** The **capitol** building is in Washington. Congress meets there to make decisions.

7-90. **capital:** Indianapolis is the **capital** of the state of Indiana. We start sentences with **capital** letters.

dessert – desert

7-91. **dessert:** Mom makes the best blackberry pies for **dessert**. I like ice cream on mine.

7-92. **desert:** It is very dry in the **desert**. Only wild flowers and cactus grow there.

flour – flower

7-93. **flour:** Mom uses **flour** to make blackberry pies for dessert. It comes in a sealed bag.

7-94. **flower:** We have some very pretty **flowers** growing in the yard.

one – won

7-95. **one:** I have only **one** brother and no sisters.

7-96. **won:** Mary **won** the school spelling contest, fair and square.

fir – fur

7-97. **fir:** There is a beautiful green **fir** tree in our yard. It is an evergreen. It is green all year round.

7-98. **fur:** My new winter jacket has a **fur** lining. It is made from animal **fur** and is very warm.

been – bin

7-99. **been:** Mom tells me you have **been** a good boy today.

7-100. **bin:** Dad got a sack of penny nails from the nail **bin**. A **bin** is a little box for storing things

creak – creek

7-101. **creak:** I could hear the door **creak** when my brother opened it. It *squeaked*. I need to oil it.

7-102. **creek:** Mr. Potter's dad took him swimming in the **creek**.

flea – flee

7-103. **flea:** Mom told me not to pet the dog because he has **fleas**. A **flea** is a *little bug that jumps* to get around.

7-104. **flee:** We knew to **flee** from the dog when we saw he had **fleas**. To **flee** is to *run away from danger*.

hair – hare

7-105. **hair:** My dad's **hair** is getting white. He says it makes him look distinguished.

7-106. **hare:** We fed the **hare** in the backyard a carrot. A **hare** looks like a big rabbit with long ears.

heal – heel

7-107. **heal:** The doctor said he could **heal** the sick boy. He would make him well.

7-108. **heel:** I have worn these shoes so long that the **heels** are falling off.

mail – male

7-109. **mail:** The **mail** came early today. I got a letter from John.

7-110. **male:** I got a **male** puppy today. It is a little boy dog.

marry – merry

7-111. **marry:** Jim and Alice are going to **marry** today.

7-112. **merry:** We had a **merry** time at the fair. We had great fun!

meet – meat

7-113. **meat:** Chicken is my favorite **meat**. I like my chicken baked.

7-114. **meet:** It is nice to **meet** you. I am glad to get to know you.

pain – pane

7-115. **pain:** Jack felt a lot of **pain** in his arm when he fell out of the tree.

7-116. **pane:** We put a new window **pane** in the old window to keep the cold wind out.

patience - patients

7-117. **patience:** My teacher had a lot of **patience** with me. She always helped me and never got angry.

7-118. **patients:** A lot of people are sick today. We have a lot of **patients** in the hospital.

beech – beach

7-119. **beech:** The **beech** tree is a large tree with smooth gray leaves and glassy leaves. Wild birds like the beechnut fruit that grows on the **beech** tree.

7-120. **beach:** My family likes to go the **beach** to swim.

principal – principle

7-121. principal: Mr. Albert Potter was Donald Potter's **principal** when he was in school.

7-122. principle: The alphabet is the first **principle** of reading. It is the foundation for good reading.

tail – tale

7-123. tail: The dog had a long **tail**.

7-124. tale: A **tale** is a story. I love the **tale** of the Hobbit Frodo and the One Ring.

war – wore

7-125. war: The men fought bravely for their country in the **war**.

7-126. wore: I **wore** my heavy jacket because it was cold out yesterday.

A Brief History of the Development

of *Beyond Blend Phonics*

From the Author

I first developed *Beyond Blend Phonics: English Morphology Made Easy* in December of 2011 as a series of Power Point slides to be used with my tutoring students who had finished my *Blend Phonics Lessons and Stories*. *Beyond Blend Phonics* takes the students beyond the basic decoding skills into advanced levels of word identification and usage. The slides proved to be very effective so I decided to publish them in this book format to reach a wider audience and help more students.

My *Blend Phonics Lessons and Stories* is an original work based on the phonics sequence (hierarchy of skills) in Hazel Logan Loring's 1980 *Reading Made Easy with Blend Phonics for First Grade*. Mrs. Elizabeth Brown wrote 61 stories to go with the lessons, and I added comprehension questions, spelling words and one extra story. This easy-to-teach program has proven highly effective with beginning and remedial students. My *Blend Phonics Lessons and Stories* or a similar high quality phonics-first reading program should be thoroughly mastered before beginning *Beyond Blend Phonics*.

Beyond Blend Phonics was inspired by Dr. Marcia L. Henry's 1991 paper, "Organizing Decoding Instruction." It was published in *All Language and the Creation of Literacy* by the Orton Dyslexia Society. Dr. Henry's essay offered an intellectual alternative (antidote) to the popular Whole Language method that was negatively impacting reading instruction at that time. Dr. Henry explained how students can improve their reading ability by receiving direct instruction in the Three Layers or Levels of English that are based on the language of origin: Anglo-Saxon, Romance (Latin & French), and Greek.

I would like to recommend two other books by Dr. Henry: *Unlocking Literacy: Effective Decoding and Spelling Instruction* is a comprehensive college level textbook covering every aspect of literacy development. The second book, *Words: Integrating Decoding Instruction Based on Word Origin and Word Structure,* is a fully articulated curriculum teaching the three levels of English. I have taught *WORDS* to my advanced tutoring students for over a decade.

This document was published with CreateSpace on March 12, 2015. On July 17, 2017 a major revision was made to give preference to syllable boundaries over morpheme boundaries. My heartfelt appreciation is due to my proofreader, Kathy Gonzalez, of Australia. Last update: Jan. 24, 2018.

The Levels of Language – Historical Overview

English has been influenced by other languages. It did not originate in England as you might think. The oldest words came from tribes who invaded England from northern Europe and wiped out the civilization they found there.

These **Anglo-Saxon** conquerors had few words, mostly those connected with things they used and actions of their daily lives. This Old English resembled German; many of the words we use today came from Anglo-Saxon. Most of our one-syllable words are Anglo-Saxon, words like <u>bed</u>, <u>cold</u>, <u>sit</u>, <u>but</u>, <u>milk</u>, <u>field</u>, <u>walk</u>, and <u>eat</u>.

Norman invaders came later (1066) from what is now called France. Their language contained many words they had learned from the Romans, who at one time conquered France. The language of the Romans was called Latin; we have many words that were originally Latin. This is the **Romance Level** of English.

Later, again, scholars in England borrowed words directly from Latin itself, which for centuries was the language of the educated men and women all over Europe. Many of our longer and more scholarly words reached us in this way, words like <u>illustrate</u>, <u>transportation</u>, <u>speculate</u>. Henry tells us, "The Latin word roots are probably the most productive elements for students to learn. These roots are relatively easy to learn and are important for enhancing vocabulary as well as decoding. James I. Brown suggested that by teaching just 14 master words containing 12 Latin roots and 2 Greek roots, students could learn tens of thousands of words."

The Romans themselves borrowed many words from the **Greeks**. Some of the Greek words had themselves been borrowed from still earlier people, the Phoenicians. Greek words entered English by the thousands during the Renaissance to meet the needs of scholars and scientists. Letter-sound correspondences are similar to Anglo-Saxon and Romance-based words, but words of Greek origin commonly use the sounds of /k/ for ch, /f/ for ph, and /ĭ/ for y/ as in <u>chlorophyll</u>. Other common combinations are /n/ for pn in <u>pneumonia</u>, /m/ for m in mn=<u>mnemonics</u>, and and /r/ for rh in rhetoric. Today we use many words from Greek, including <u>philosophy</u>, <u>microscope</u>, <u>physiology</u>, and <u>hydrometer</u>. This is called the **Greek Level**.

The Story of English

I. Simple English: Mostly Anglo-Saxon

A long time ago there was a place that had no name. It was filled with men and women who could not do a lot of things. They could hunt deer. They could stand still and hide. They might kick a cat or pet the dog. They ran fast, and played games and built houses. They might stop and start or jump up and down with joy. They had no bats to swing or balls to hit. Yet they did shout and scream and laugh and cry. To get food to eat, they would spear fish and grow plants. They got milk from cows. They cut down trees to make houses. They grew grapes and made wine. At night they could watch the moon and stars. Or they could just go to sleep. Then came some men in big boats from a place called Rome.

Flesch Kincaid Grade Level: 2.0

II. Fancy English: Mostly Latin and French

This place is what today we call **England**. When the **Roman legions conquered** this island they **considered** the **indigenous** people **savages** who were **completely** without **culture** and **legal traditions**. **Naturally** they had to **educate** them. Since these **savages** had no **legal** terms or **cultural** terms in their **vocabulary**, the Romans added the **necessary** words from their own **language,** which was **Latin**. **Eventually missionaries** from **Ireland** and **Italy** brought **Christianity** to these **pagans**. These **missionaries** taught the **savages** that if they changed their **religion** from **polytheism**, were **baptized**, and **accepted Jesus** as their **savior, salvation** could be theirs. Because the **savages** did not have the **appropriate** words in their simple story telling **language**, the **missionaries** added the words or **created** words from their two **favorite languages**, **Latin** and Greek. Then came the **Norman** French. They **conquered** the somewhat **civilized savages** and added to their **vocabulary** words dealing with **cuisine** and **military matters**. So now words like **victuals, lieutenant, colonel, bivouac, rendezvous, boudoir,** and **unique** were added to the **language**. And as **foreign** words **entered** the **language** they kept their **phonetic patterns** rather than changing to the **phonic** spelling of the **original story**-telling **language** of the **savages**.

Flesch Kincaid Grade Level: 11.0

Notice how the levels of English dramatically affect reading levels. *Beyond Blend Phonics* is designed to improve reading ability by directly teaching the spelling patterns (orthographic structures or morphemes) for each Level.

English Vocabulary: Origins

Decile	English	French	Latin	Danish	Other
1	83%	11%	2%	2%	2%
2	34	46	11	2	7
3	29	46	14	1	10
4	27	45	17	1	10
5	27	47	17	1	8
6	27	42	19	2	10
7	23	45	17	2	13
8	26	41	18	2	13
9	25	41	17	2	15
10	25	42	18	1	14

Explanation: If we group the vocabulary of English into the first most frequent thousand words, second most frequent thousand words, third most frequent thousand words, and so on, then compute the percentage of native versus borrowed words in each of these groups of a thousand, we find the above figures.

The "other" group includes mostly mixed or doubtful words, or words that only might be assigned to English, French or Latin words. Only Dutch among "other" exceeds 1 percent in any of the deciles). When all the words are in running text are put into one group, the percentages are as follows: English 78.1; French 15.2; Latin 3.1; Danish 2.4; other (Greek, Dutch, Italian, Spanish, German, etc.): 1.3. Comment. These data were compiled from several thousand business letters. (Roberts, A. Hood. *A Statistical Linguistic Analysis of American English*. The Hague, 1965.) From Williams, Joseph M. *Origins of the English Language, A Social and Linguistic History*. The Free Press, 1975.

The English column represents words of Anglo-Saxon origin. Note that after thest most frequent thousand words, words of Romance origin become more frequent than Anglo-Saxon words. *Beyond Blend Phonics: English Morphology Made Easy* is a powerful yet simple tool for boosting students' reading vocabulary.

Word Count for *Beyond Blend Phonics*

Prepared by Donald L. Potter

Chapter 1: Anglo-Saxon Prefixes: 41 words

Chapter 2: Anglo-Saxon Suffixes: 58 words

Chapter 3: Romance Prefixes: 178 total words

    Section 1: (Open Syllables) 30 words

    Section 2: Closed Syllables) 70 words

    Section 3: (Disguised Prefixes) 78 words.

Chapter 4: Romance Suffixes: 110 words

Chapter 5: Romance Roots: 167 words

Chapter 6: Greek Combining Forms: 52 words

Chapter 7: Homonyms : 126 words

Total: 732 words

Instructions for Teachers and Tutors

In keeping with the ease of teaching of my *Blend Phonics Lessons and Stories*, I developed *Beyond Blend Phonics* to make it equally easy for teachers, tutors, and parents to teach the more advanced levels of English morphology. While no learning is totally free of effort, the Parallel Sentences Method for teaching the meaning of words significantly reduces the teacher's work load and dramatically increase student success.

Dr. Marcia K. Henry's important 1990 paper "Organizing Decoding Instruction" serves an excellent introduction to my approach. This approach involves organizing instruction in English morphology according language of origin. Her paper can be accessed from my website. The Three Levels according to language of origin are:

1. Anglo-Saxon prefixes and suffixes
2. Romance (Latin and French) prefixes, suffixes, and roots
3. Greek Combining forms

The program is very flexible. Any number of teaching techniques can be used. The work can be oral, written, or both.

The first sentence gives the word in context. The following sentence or sentences illustrate the meaning with a word or phrase.

The procedure is simply to have the students study the morphemes as they are presented and then read the sentences. Discuss the words to make sure the students understand and can use them. It is good, if there is time, to have the students write the words in a spiral notebook.

The program is designed to provide concentrated exposure to the morphemes of English words in meaningful sentences. Much of the learning will be by analogy, similar to the way they developed most of their vocabulary in the first place, without formal efforts to memorize the words.

The object of the program is not just to teach a select group of words, but to teach the morphemes that make up many words so students can identify and understand **other** words with the same morphemes. This can lead to a dramatic increase in vocabulary and overall reading ability.

Mr. Potter has written two handwriting programs, that are available for free on his website. *Shortcut to Manuscript* and *Shortcut to Cursive*. They are proven methods for teaching fluent handwriting.

ABOUT THE AUTHOR

Mr. Potter was a public school teacher for twenty-one years, including five years as a full time substitute teacher, fourteen years as a bilingual teacher, one year as a reading specialist, and two years as a secondary Spanish teacher. Upon retiring from public education, he began teaching at a private school in Odessa, TX. At the private school, he taught fourth grade one year and then switched to Spanish, remedial reading, and cursive handwriting.

Besides his regular teaching job, Mr. Potter also has a very busy tutoring practice. It has been his privilege to help hundreds of students of all ages to learn to read and write better.

Mr. Potter began publishing material of educational interest on his own website, www.donpotter.net, in early 2003. His website is one of the richest resources for educational material available anywhere on the Internet. His website includes material of a theoretical and practical nature.

He published Hazel Logan Loring's 1980 *Reading Made Easy with Blend Phonics* in 2003. In 2007 he began using it for much of his tutoring. It quickly became apparent that the method was a very powerful way to help all students improve their reading ability. The program is very simple to teach and master, yet incredibly powerful.

Mr. Potter has four children: three girls and one boy. They are all married with families of their own. Mr. Potter loves teaching his grandchildren with his books.

Mr. Potter has several hobbies, including: mountain biking, playing guitar and harmonica, Pilates, reading, writing, and publishing.

Among Mr. Potter's published works available on Amazon and Barnes and Nobles are *Word Mastery: Phonics for the First Three Grades*; *Noah Webster's Spelling Book Method for Teaching Reading and Writing*; *Blend Phonics Lessons and Stories*; *Reading Made Easy with Blend Phonics: Plus Blend Phonics Fluency Drills*; *Blend Phonics Timed Fluency Drills*; *Psalms Reader*; *First Readers Anthology*; and *A Grammar of the Greek New Testament for Beginners*.

Made in the USA
Middletown, DE
23 February 2021